A NE
GU
JACK RUSSELL TERRIERS

JG-150

Overleaf: A Jack Russell Terrier adult and puppies.

Opposite page: A short-haired Jack Russell Terrier owned by Will Hahn.

The publisher wishes to acknowledge the following owners of the dogs in this book: Mike Bilbo, Linda C. Bollinger, Marge and Bill Brubaker, Ken Chambers, Becky Crosse, Jennifer Frank, William Hahn, Roland and Mary Hartley, Dr. and Mrs. Dwight Henninger, Katy Johnson, Lynn and Mike Kelley, Paul and Debbie McWilliams, Ed and Janet Nugent, Pete and Linda Reifel, Cheryl Robinson, Vicki Rodman, Pat Scanlan, Pam Simmons, and Peggy O. Swager.

Photographers: Linda C. Bollinger, Ken Chambers, William Hahn, Roland and Mary Hartley, Katy Johnson, Pete and Linda Reifel, Vicki Rodman, Pat Scanlan, and Pam Simmons.

The author acknowledges the contribution of Judy Iby for the following chapters in this book: Sport of Purebred Dogs, Health Care, Identification and Finding the Lost Dog, Traveling with Your Dog, and Behavior and Canine Communication.

Distributed in the UNITED STATES to the Pet Trade by T.F.H. Publications, Inc., One T.F.H. Plaza, Neptune City, NJ 07753; on the Internet at www.tfh.com; in CANADA Rolf C. Hagen Inc., 3225 Sartelon St. Laurent-Montreal Quebec H4R 1E8; Pet Trade by H & L Pet Supplies Inc., 27 Kingston Crescent, Kitchener, Ontario N2B 2T6; in ENGLAND by T.F.H. Publications, PO Box 15, Waterlooville PO7 6BQ; in AUSTRALIA AND THE SOUTH PACIFIC by T.F.H. (Australia), Pty. Ltd., Box 149, Brookvale 2100 N.S.W., Australia; in NEW ZEALAND by Brooklands Aquarium Ltd. 5 McGiven Drive, New Plymouth, RD1 New Zealand; in SOUTH AFRICA, Rolf C. Hagen S.A. (PTY.) LTD. P.O. Box 201199, Durban North 4016, South Africa; in Japan by T.F.H. Publications, Japan—Jiro Tsuda, 10-12-3 Ohjidai, Sakura, Chiba 285, Japan. Published by T.F.H. Publications, Inc.
MANUFACTURED IN THE
UNITED STATES OF AMERICA
BY T.F.H. PUBLICATIONS, INC.

A NEW OWNER'S GUIDE TO
JACK RUSSELL TERRIERS

LINDA C. BOLLINGER
&
PEGGY O. SWAGER

Contents

1998 Edition

This quartet of Jack Russells proudly poses for posterity.

Choose a puppy that is alert and active, with bright eyes and a shining coat.

Jack Russell Terriers are excellent hunting dogs.

The Jack Russell Terrier's loving and happy disposition makes him the ideal family pet.

Jack Russell Terriers excel in agility competition.

HISTORY of the Jack Russell Terrier

"Brothers and Sisters, I bid you beware of giving your heart to a dog to tear."—Rudyard Kipling

The Jack Russell Terrier seems to be the vogue dog for the '90s. Celebrities, as well as the average Joe, have been seen with them in increasing numbers. This small but tough terrier is working hard in show business, appearing as Milo in the movie *The Mask* and Eddie in the television sitcom *Frasier*. A Jack Russell named Wishbone is the male lead character in a children's television show that teaches children about classic literature. Numerous Jack Russell Terriers have appeared in commercials, advertising everything from new cars to pretzels and beer.

One of the first things people notice about these dogs is how clever and well trained they are. But anyone who investigates this breed is in for a surprise. Although the Jack Russell Terrier is quick to learn, his sense of self-importance makes *Parson Jack Russell, who lived in Devonshire, England in the 19th century, was an avid collector of terriers and developed the breed named after him.* him, at times, stubborn and hard to deal with. This quality is beneficial for hunting because the dog works by himself going into tunnels that lead to the prey's den. These terriers are very adaptable and form strong bonds with people, however, owners need to be aware that the dog has mental and physical demands that must be met. Although called a breed, they are more accurately a strain or type of terrier due to breeding practices that allow for a large diversity in the dog. A good way to start to understand this breed is through his history.

The Jack Russell Terrier is often called the Parson's Jack Russell Terrier. The origination of the breed is attributed to Parson John (aka Jack) Russell of Great Britain. The Parson selectively bred these dogs to develop a good fox hunting terrier. As the story goes, the Parson supposedly purchased a fox terrier-type dog between 1815 and 1819 (there is not an

agreement on the actual date). He named the female dog Trump, and she was the progenitor of the Parson's legendary terriers. Trump's characteristics that most appealed to the Parson were her size and proportions in comparison to that of a fox. Trump was said to be 14 inches at the shoulder, which is approximately the same size as a full-grown vixen (a female fox). With fox hunting in mind, the Parson wanted a terrier that could keep up with the foxhound pack and fit down a fox hole to flush out the prey for the hounds to continue chasing. Trump was said to be mostly white, having only brown patches over each ear and eye, and a penny-sized spot at the root of her tail. Her coat was thick and had a slightly wire-haired texture.

The Jack Russell Terrier is a "go-to-ground" breed, perfect for flushing small game out of its burrows during hunting.

The Parson was said to be an obsessional fox hunter. He was quite insistent that the terrier should not be required to thrash, cripple, or kill the fox. The terriers were to nip and tease the fox to get it to bolt from its den. The Parson bred for what he called gentlemanly characteristics in his strain. Over the years, a lot of small, white-haired, working terriers were called Jack Russells, though all may not have descended from the original stock.

Years later, the rise of a shorter breed of Jack Russell Terrier was thought to have occurred, in part, because of some people's preference to hunting game smaller than the English fox. The longer legs were not needed because the dog was not running with the horses and hounds. Some of these Jack Russell Terriers were used in the sport of rat killing. Rat killing was popular in the early part of the 20th century in England. The sport dealt with penning a large number of rats, then throwing in a dog to see how many rats the dog could kill and how quickly he could do it. Some Jack Russell dogs were thought to have been crossed with Bull Terriers to develop more competitive dogs. Today, however, the Jack Russell Terrier Club of America (JRTCA)

The Jack Russell Terrier was developed to meet the needs of hunters in 19th century England.

standard does not accept dogs that show Bull Terrier crossing. Dogs that excelled at this sport had a gameness and were close to the ground in their conformation for killing efficiency.

Another modification of the breed was believed more predominant in the northern part of England. The terrain in the northern part of England was rocky, and fox hunting was often done on foot instead of horseback. Because hunters couldn't dig the fox out through the rock, the terrier dogs were bred to be more aggressive in order to tackle the fox and drag it out.

Unfortunately, for many years neither the original taller nor the modified shorter types of Jack Russells were looked upon with any enthusiasm. In the mid 1970s, the Jack Russell Terrier Club of Great Britain was formed. The club had loose standards for registration and attempted to weed out dogs that had backs that were too long, crooked fronts, and stand-up ears. The desired terrier was one that possessed the well-balanced show proportions of the original Trump.

The establishment of Jack Russell Terriers in America is credited to a gift puppy named Rare, given from Mrs. Nelson Slater to Mrs. Harden Crawford III around 1960. Mrs. Crawford

This puppy resembles one of the first Jack Russell Terriers; a fox-terrier type dog with brown patches over the eyes, ears, and on the root of her tail.

became interested in the breed and acquired more of the dogs from England. Mrs. Crawford went on to found the Jack Russell Terrier Club of America (JRTCA). She also helped to set down guidelines for the breed, which helps to protect the breed from poor breeding practices. There are two clubs for Jack Russell Terrier registrations; the first, the JRTCA and the second club, the JRTBA (Jack Russell Terrier Breeder's Association). The JRTBA filed for AKC registration, They are now known as the JRTAA.

REGISTRATION

When you make the decision to own a Jack Russell Terrier, there will be many clubs and registries of which you will need to be aware. To the average first-time dog owner, these may seem like a lot of meaningless initials and the clubs' significance should be defined.

The oldest Jack Russell Terrier registry is the Jack Russell Terrier Club of America (JRTCA). This registry was founded from the Jack Russell Terrier Club of Great Britain (JRTCGB). A group of people broke away from the JRTCA and started the Jack Russell Terrier Breeder's Association (JRTBA), which later applied for American Kennel Club (AKC) registry.

The Jack Russell Terrier made his first appearance in the United States as recently as 1960. Little Bag of Peanuts owned by Dave and Katy Johnson.

All of these clubs deal with dog registry. Registry will dictate in which shows your Jack Russell can participate. If you are interested in only owning a pet, then registry helps guarantee that the dog is purebred. So how can a new pet owner decide which registry is significant for his needs? Since the JRTBA is now represented by AKC registry and the JRTCGB is really meant for people in England, the AKC and the JRTCA registries are the two that need to be examined.

The AKC is a well-known dog registry organization and is responsible for sponsoring the biggest dog show in the US, the Westminster Kennel Club show in New York City. Because of this event, people automatically equate AKC registry with champions and good breeding. Unfortunately, this is misleading. AKC registry does not guarantee a quality puppy.

When the AKC recognizes a new breed like the Jack Russell Terrier, it begins by accepting applications for terriers from several breeders. These applicants must meet specific breed standards. From November 1, 1997 to November 1, 2000, Jack Russell Terriers that meet the registry requirements will be accepted for registration. These Jack Russells must already be registered with an acceptable domestic registry and have a complete three-generation pedigree. The AKC height standard for the Jack Russell is between 12 and 14 inches. After November 1, 2000, the registration will be closed. After that time, the only way a Jack Russell Terrier can be registered is if he is born to parents that are AKC registered.

The JRTCA has been in existence since the 1960s. Their books were closed long ago. Like the AKC, they started the registry by being selective about the dogs that were accepted. The JRTCA registers Jack Russell Terriers that are 10 to 15 inches tall. The JRTCA believes in breeding the smaller size because the emphasis of the club is on perpetuating a working terrier that can hunt, and the smaller size allows the dog to enter smaller dens to flush out the prey.

Both clubs offer shows in which people can enter their dogs. The JRTCA calls their shows "trials" and these trials are less formal than AKC shows. The major difference between the two clubs is in the quality of the offspring of the registered dogs. The JRTCA has a registry system that helps to safeguard against genetic defects and offspring that no longer meet the breed standard.

The JRTCA's strict registration process does not accept a terrier for registration until the dog is one year of age and has passed a veterinarian's exam. This process ensures that the adult terrier meets the breed's conformational standards, has a complete pedigree, and is free of genetic defects. For the dog breeder, these are very high standards; for the buyer, this is an assurance of a quality dog. Although there is a risk that the purebred dog will not meet the breed standards, there is a guarantee that at least the parents were of breed standard quality and free of certain genetic defects. With AKC-registered dogs, the puppies can have genetic defects or not meet with the standards that define the breed and still be registered and bred to produce more puppies, allowing for the perpetuation of dangerous genetic defects. Although "AKC registered" is deemed to be a stamp of quality when buying a dog, it actually does not ensure the conformational quality or physical health of the animal. Several AKC-registered breeds have suffered from poor breeding by unknowledgeable breeders or those who desire to breed and sell purely for profit. AKC registration does not ruin Jack Russells, however, poor breeding practices do, which is why the JRTCA safeguards against this. Also, the JRTCA adheres to breeding for hunting purposes, which adds to the personality that makes this little dog so endearing.

For a person interested in owning a Jack Russell Terrier, the two registries can be confusing. Unless you plan on showing your dog, the main purpose of acquiring a registered dog is to ensure that you have purchased a purebred Jack Russell Terrier. If the dog you are considering is AKC registered, you may need to do more checking to be sure that the parents and the puppy are free from genetic defects and meet current breed standards. Although the JRTCA has a system that helps to ensure health and quality, all puppies need to be purchased on their own merit.

The Jack Russell Terrier Club of America sponsors many breed appropriate events each year in which dog and owner can participate.

PORTRAIT of the Jack Russell Terrier

Jack Russell Terriers have several of the qualities we admire in our heroes. They are tough, determined, devoted, dedicated, and loyal to a fault. They are also extremely clever, feisty, intelligent, and attentive to their owners. When you talk to many people who know Jack Russells, it is easy to get the sense of the love/hate phenomenon. The people who are incompatible with the Jack Russell usually do not end up owning them for long. This has created a need for Jack Russell rescue organizations that are offered through the breed registries. These rescue operations work hard to place the unwanted Jack Russell Terrier in a more appropriate home.

People who happily own Jack Russells have unlimited stories about how wonderful these pets are. Happy owners go on like proud parents do with their children. Instead of a list of phenomenal accomplishments, they tell the cute antics of their clever and darling dog. Needless to say, this dog is not for everyone.

The Jack Russell Terrier is an active intelligent companion, but is not suited to every lifestyle. They require plenty of exercise, mental challenges, and discipline.

One of the keys to successfully owning a Jack Russell Terrier is to acknowledge they aren't like many "classic" family dogs. This dog must have exercise, play, mental challenges, and discipline. Although the Jack Russell Terrier learns quickly, the dog often considers his own opinion more important than his owner's. Needless to say, the dog must be trained to obey the owner's wishes. Getting a Jack Russell to obey often takes longer than many other breeds. Never use harsh punishment to teach your dog to obey. Success comes from making the dog do the task until the dog realizes he has no choice in the matter. The owner must persist until the dog does the task every time. At the same time, the owner must understand that there is a fine line between repetition and boring the dog to death. Eventually, the dog accepts the fact that he might as well do what has been asked right away, so he can get on to what he thinks is important.

For potential Jack Russell Terrier owners who do not want to be bothered by the mandatory training, this is not a good breed. If the owner doesn't train the dog, the dog will train the owner. These terriers can become tyrants with their owners and make their owner's lives miserable, earning them the nickname "Jack Russell Terrorists." A Jack Russell Terrier is an intense worker with seemingly endless energy. Owners don't want them in charge.

A well-raised Jack Russell Terrier can learn that their owners are intelligent creatures. But because the dog has been bred to hunt in dark holes where he makes life and death decisions, he will always have an opinion on everything. Even the well-trained dog that played Milo (real name, Max) in the movie *The Mask* was known to add his interpretation to a scene when doing the movie. In a scene with a Frisbee, Max decided not to let go of the Frisbee right away, because he felt a tug-of-war would be more fun. His trainer had no problem with Max adding his own interpretation, but if this wouldn't have worked, they would have had to reshoot the scene and have Max do it the original way. The trainer knew how to monopolize the Jack Russell Terrier's desire to please his owners, and therefore, the dog could be made to perform exactly as he was told.

Jack Russell Terriers do not see themselves as small dogs. In their mind, they are among the largest breeds, and they have the mentality to match. A dog standing next to them may make the Jack Russell appear like a dwarf, but that large dog will not intimidate the Jack Russell, and the Jack Russell will not

The Jack Russell Terrier has been bred to hunt in dark holes where he must make life and death decisions.

hesitate to attack first if the terrier sees the need. In fact, the Jack Russell is often known to be aggressive with other dogs. They are also aggressive with each other. Problems with same-sex aggression are well documented in this breed. There is no guarantee that more than one of each sex can be safely kept together. Fights to the death have occurred between females. Some people have reported that males and females altered at an early age are more sociable, but, because of their temperament, there is no guarantee that two

A Jack Russell Terrier is an intense worker with seemingly endless energy.

No animal, no matter how large, will intimidate the courageous Jack Russell Terrier.

dogs of this breed can be safely kept together unattended.

Some of the other traits that make this dog a great hunter are his digging ability, his ability to bay (a deep, prolonged bark) and bark, his tenacious and assertive nature, and his ability to follow a scent. These dogs are bred to go into the ground following a scent, bark or bay at the quarry, and sometimes dig it out. They will often nip and tease until the animal bolts, and some will grab the prey and drag it out. All of these wonderful abilities become an owner's torment when the dog is bored, underexercised, or

Jack Russell Terriers are energetic, highly intelligent, affectionate animals that need constant activity and companionship to be happy.

undisciplined. When the breed is left alone for long hours, unoccupied, they have been known to be destructive chewers or bark endlessly at nothing in general. Often they will dig out of a backyard, or climb or jump a fence. Some will occupy themselves digging all over the yard. They will invent fun jobs for themselves, like taunting and bullying children and guests. Sometimes they will decide to be guardian of the world and their possessions. They will chase cats, hunt birds, and if given the chance, chase cars. However, when appropriately matched with their owners, these dogs are loyal, affectionate, and make the greatest companions an owner could ever have. People who love their Jack Russell Terriers often do so because they are highly intelligent dogs that enjoy human interaction. As Gene Hackman's character put it in the movie *Crimson Tide,* "These are the smartest damn dogs in the world."

PHYSICAL APPEARANCE

There are three coat types in the Jack Russell Terrier: smooth, rough, and broken. A smooth coat should be thick and straight, showing fair length and density to provide a good body covering. After running your hand over the coat, it will have a texture that some people

The Jack Russell's superior ability to dig is one of the characteristics that have made him a great hunting dog.

describe as greasy. A short or fine coat is uncharacteristic, as well as a hard crinkly coat, especially along the line of the back. Smooth coats do not have any indication of whiskers around the face. Their coat should never be so sparse as to not provide protection from the elements or so fine that it is uncharacteristic.

A rough coat should only be a trifle wiry, but not overly hard, crinkly, or wavy. A rough coat should not be fine or linty in texture. The rough coat has more texture to the hair, but is never woolly.

The broken coat is a combination of both smooth and rough coats. This coat can have longer hairs mixed with the shorter ones. With a broken coat, parts of the body may be smooth, such as the head, legs, or chest. It is not uncommon for a broken coat to have a fuzzy muzzle or longer hair on the legs. A broken coat can vary from just slightly broken to a more predominantly broken coat.

Ricochet Annie, Bowery Buck, Horsemaster's Tiggeruni, and Tansy Ragwort of Safe Chase are all perfect examples of the different coat types and markings of the Jack Russell Terrier.

The Jack Russell Terrier Club of America states that the height range for a full-grown Jack Russell should be between 10 and 15 inches.

All of the coat types have an undercoat; however, even the rough-coated Jack Russells do not have enough undercoat to survive out in the cold.

Because this is a small dog with either a short or a longer wiry coat, a lot of people seem to assume the dog doesn't shed much. Actually, the smooth variety sheds the most. Because this dog seems to drop hair all year round, the owner needs to plan on regular brushing and a lot of vacuuming to control the problem.

The JRTBA states the height range for the Jack Russell Terrier is between 12 and 14 inches. This is also the standard recognized by the Kennel Club in England and the United Kennel Club, whereas the JRTCGB agrees with the JRTCA standards that are stated in this book. Some people refer to the 12- to 14-inch standard as the standard for the Parson's Jack Russell, though that particular name is currently tied up in copyrights in the US. On the other hand, the JRTCA realizes that some Jack Russell Terrier breeders have bred dogs to hunt smaller prey, therefore, they recognize a height between 10 to 15 inches. Australia's registry recognizes a Jack Russell Terrier from 9 to 12 inches and a Parson's Jack Russell from 12 to 14 inches. There is one other significant difference in the registry of the two American Jack Russell Terrier clubs. That difference is in the registration of the puppies. The JRTCA registers dogs at one year of age, and each is accepted upon his own merits. The JRTBA dogs are automatically registered if their parents are registered, even if the dog is not up to breed standards.

The breed standards for the Jack Russell Terrier were developed from the function as a hunting dog. No matter what coat type, a Jack Russell Terrier should have a thick coarse outercoat and a good undercoat. This type of coat structure helps protect the dog when he goes in and out of holes in his daily work. The terrier should have a predominantly white coat. By JRTCA standards, the coat must be 51% white. The white color makes it easy to see the dog out in the field when hunting.

The back legs of the Jack Russell Terrier should be structured to form an inverted U-shape from behind. This gives the dog drive to push through a hole. A good angle of the back legs viewed from a profile and a straight back helps the dog to brace with the back legs and pull quarry out.

The distance from the front toe of the terrier to the withers should equal the distance from the withers to the base of the tail. A dog that is too long or short cannot turn around in a hole. The tail is docked to a hand-hold length so the owner can grab it and remove the dog from a hole if necessary. Also when backing out of a tunnel, the dog's tail is less likely to be painfully injured when it is shorter.

The front legs should be muscular and straight. They are designed to fold into the main body. The chest needs to be flexible and one should be able to span it with two hands. Larger and inflexible chests are considered a fault. Both

The breed standards for the Jack Russell were developed based on the desired characteristics of a hunting dog.

22

The back legs of the Jack Russell Terrier should be structured to form an inverted U-shape from behind. This gives the dog the power he needs to push through a hole after his prey.

the leg and chest design help the dog squeeze just a little smaller in tight spots.

The neck needs to be in proportion and flexible. In a tunnel, the dog may need to duck or defend against prey he has cornered. The undesirable short neck often accompanies a too-straight shoulder. The almond-shaped eyes means the skull behind will be strong and help shield against eye damage. The eyes should be dark and clear and the nose black. If the nose is not black, then the dog probably has mixed breeding. The ears need to fold over to prevent dirt from getting inside.

THE SMALL VERSUS THE TALL

The Jack Russell Terrier was bred to hunt. What the Jack Russell Terrier hunts varies from area to area and so does the size of the hole the dog must enter. Taller terriers were thought to be preferred by the Parson Jack Russell because the dog was better able to cover more miles when following a horse while on a hunt. Today, fewer people in America engage in hunting over large areas. Some are involved in hunting smaller game like rats, and the size of the terrier is not as significant. Smaller Jack Russells, ranging from 10 to 12 inches, have been bred for smaller quarry like woodchucks. Regardless of the size of the individual dog, what is important is the proportion. The length of the dog should not exceed the dog's height at the shoulder.

No matter what the size, the Jack Russell Terrier should be well balanced. There is a type of Jack Russell Terrier that is short and unbalanced. The main conformation faults include a dog that is under 10 inches, has short legs that are often crooked, has a long back, and a wide chest. These dogs are playfully nicknamed "Puddin" dogs.

No matter what the size of the Jack Russell Terrier, he must be a well-balanced dog.

This dog's short legs and long body are characteristic of a "Puddin" Jack Russell Terrier.

PUDDINS

"Puddin" is a nickname for a specific type of Jack Russell Terrier. These terriers are not registerable through any club because of conformation faults. Some people say that Puddins are more gentle and less active than true Jack Russells, but they can vary as much in personality and energy level as the registerable Jack Russells.

A Puddin has a body all out of proportion. The body is longer than the dog is tall at the shoulder. A true Puddin has short bowed legs. The short bowed front legs are due to a genetic problem called achondroplasia. Achondroplasia causes cartilage to abnormally converge into bone. The result is a dwarfism apparent at birth. With this mutation, the dog's extremities are short, but not their trunk. This is a dominant genetic trait, which means it is easily passed along when breeding. Though some Puddins are taller and have straighter legs, they still have a body that is too long for registration. The reason these dogs are rejected goes back to the function of the breed. Too long a body keeps the dog from hunting. Puddins cannot enter conformation classes, but can compete in other events at Jack Russell Terrier shows.

STANDARD for the JRTCA Jack Russell Terrier

CHARACTERISTICS—The terrier must present a lively, active, and alert appearance. It should impress with its fearless and happy disposition. It should be remembered that the Jack Russell is a working terrier and should retain these instincts. Nervousness, cowardice, or over-aggressiveness should be discouraged. The terrier should always appear confident.

GENERAL APPEARANCE—This is a sturdy tough terrier, very much on its toes all the time, measuring between 10 and 15 inches at the withers. The body length must be in proportion to the height, and should present a compact, balanced image, always being in solid, and in hard condition.

The Jack Russell Terrier must possess the strength and ability to work over any type of terrain.

HEAD—Should be well balanced and in proportion to the body. The skull should be flat, or moderate width at the ears, narrowing to the eyes. There should be a definite stop, but the stop should not be over pronounced. The length of muzzle from the nose to the stop should be slightly shorter than the distance from the stop to the occiput (the back of the skull). The nose should be black. The jaw should be powerful and well boned with strongly muscled cheeks.

EYES—Should be almond shaped, dark in color and full of life and intelligence.

EARS—Should be small, "V" shaped, drop ears carried forward close to the head and of moderate thickness.

The clean-cut lines of the head of the Jack Russell Terrier are distinctive in this breed. A good head has almond-shaped eyes and fold-down ears.

MOUTH–Strong teeth with the top slightly overlapping the lower. A level bite is acceptable for registration.

NECK–Clean and muscular, of good length, gradually widening at the shoulders.

FOREQUARTERS–The shoulders should be sloping and well laid back, and should be fine at points and clearly cut at the withers. Forelegs should be strong and straight boned with joints in correct alignment. Elbows should hang perpendicular to the body and work free of the sides.

BODY–The chest should be shallow and narrow, and the front legs should not be set too widely apart. The dog should have an athletic, rather than heavily chested appearance. As a guide only, the chest should be small enough to be easily spanned behind the shoulders, by average-sized hands, when the terrier is in a fit, working condition. The back should be strong, straight and, in comparison to the height of the terrier, it should give a balanced image. The loin should be slightly arched.

HINDQUARTERS—Should be strong and muscular, well put together with good angulation and bend of stifle, giving plenty of drive and propulsion. Looking from behind, the hocks must be straight.

FEET—Round, hard padded, of cat-like appearance, neither turning in or out.

TAIL—Should be set rather high, carried gaily and in proportion to body length. The tail is usually cut to about four inches long, which provides a good hand-hold.

COAT—Smooth coats should not be so sparse as not to provide a certain amount of protection from the elements and undergrowth. Rough or broken coats should not be woolly.

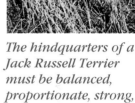

The hindquarters of a Jack Russell Terrier must be balanced, proportionate, strong, and muscular.

COLOR—White should predominate (must be more than 50% white) with tan, black, or brown markings. Brindle markings are unacceptable.

GAIT—Movement should be free, lively, and well coordinated with straight action in front and behind.

SHOWING PURPOSES—For showing purposes, terriers are classified into two groups: 10 to 12 $^1/_2$ inches, and 12 $^1/_2$ to 15 inches. Old scars or injuries, the result of work or accident, should not be allowed to prejudice a terrier's chance in the show ring unless they interfere with its movement or with its utility for work or stud. Male animals should have two apparently normal testicles fully descended into the scrotum. A Jack Russell Terrier should not show any strong characteristics of another breed.

FAULTS—Shyness. Disinterest. Overly aggressive. Defects in bite. Weak jaws. Fleshy ears. Down at shoulder. Barrel ribs. Out at elbow. Narrow hips. Straight stifles. Weak feet. Sluggish or unsound movement. Dishing. Plaiting. Toeing. Silky or woolly coats. Too much color (less than 51% white). Shrill or weak voice. Lack of muscle or skin tone. Lack of stamina or lung reserve. Evidence of foreign blood.

The Jack Russell Terrier must present a lively, inquisitive, and alert appearance.

SELECTING the Right Jack Russell Terrier for You

The Jack Russell Terrier is a great dog. The way to preserve the best of this terrier's characteristics is through educated buying. Potential pet owners must demand that the breeders be conscientious. There is no room for breeders who produce bad-quality dogs just to meet the sudden popularity of the breed. These types of breeding practices in the past have resulted in rampant genetic defects and the destruction of what originally attracted people to the breed.

THE RIGHT DOG FOR YOU

What makes the ideal Jack Russell Terrier varies for each owner. The owner needs to evaluate what kind of career their dog will have. Will this be the family pet, a hunter, or a trial dog, or is he expected to fit all three needs? If all three are desired, then which one is the most important? For instance, Linda Bollinger of Grealoch Jack Russell Terriers bought Springcroft Kelsey for her breeding program. Linda's main emphasis was to raise Jack Russells that hunt well, but also have a good disposition. Kelsey does great in hunting and in competition for go-to-ground. Kelsey has a boldness about entering the holes, and she is instinctive at baying when she meets a caged animal for the first time. Kelsey is also affectionate and nonaggressive with people. She loves to play, go for walks, and is very devoted to her owner. Linda chose her dog, Outback Keegan, because he has, among other things, an exceptional disposition. Keegan is less stubborn than the typical Jack Russell, more devoted, and is quiet and well behaved in public. Keegan was easier to train than most Jack Russells. He also shows ability at agility, trailing and locating, and racing.

People who hunt with Jack Russells have varying views about the value of boldness. Some terrier owners want a dog

Be sure to do your homework and learn all you can about the breed before making the decision to bring a Jack Russell Terrier into your life.

that doesn't hesitate, others prefer a dog that uses discretion, keeping him from running head first into the jaws and claws of wild animals. Some Jack Russell Terriers do not show as much natural ability for hunting. This kind of dog may be shy for going to ground.

Some Jack Russell breeders have concentrated on selecting dogs that are superior for the racing events, others may want a specific size hunting dog to be able to handle the type of game in their area. When seeking a Jack Russell, potential owners need to be sure the breeder has paid adequate attention to disposition of the dog in their breeding program.

With any breeding program, there are always individual dogs produced that will not be champions or meet the breeder's hunting needs. If a pet-quality dog is desired, more compromises in conformation can be acceptable. Pet-quality dogs shouldn't be bred, however, or the superior qualities of the breed will be lost.

A Jack Russell Terrier should never be bought from a pet shop. Reputable breeders of good Jack Russells will not release dogs to pet shops for sale because selling through pet shops is forbidden by the JRTCA. If you want to find out about the different breeders of Jack Russell Terriers, you can contact the JRTCA or the other breed club. The JRTCA puts out a monthly magazine called *True Grit* and they publish a breeder's directory.

When you contact a breeder, feel free to interview him and evaluate his answers. Let him tell you about his dogs, and what he feels are the dog's important aspects. Breeders are often very helpful in locating the right dog for you. A lot of the Jack

Whether searching for a pet-quality or show-quality Jack Russell, your breeder will help you choose the puppy that best meets your needs.

Russell Terrier breeders are members of the JRTCA and have agreed to the stringent ethics of that club.

When possible, it is a good idea to see the parents of the puppy you are going to buy. This can give a potential owner some idea of what attributes the puppy will inherit.

If local Jack Russell breeders do not have the type of terrier you want, breeders from other parts of the country can be contacted. Puppies can be shipped from anywhere. Frequently, breeders will send a pedigree and photos or a video of their dogs. A lot of the

When searching for a Jack Russell Terrier puppy, research as many breeders as possible and avoid making a hasty decision.

Your Jack Russell Terrier will have a good start in life if his parents are happy and well adjusted. Make sure to see the dam and sire of the puppy you are considering.

breeders will openly and honestly discuss their dogs' dispositions, as well as other pros and cons of each puppy, but the buyer must ask.

Some breeders offer guarantees that the puppy will be free of genetic defects or they will refund your money or replace the dog with another. Of course, if the dog begins to show signs of some of these genetic defects, the owner will have had the dog long enough to love him and usually will want to keep him anyway.

If it is possible, go to trials and meet Jack Russell people. Sometimes prospective owners can enlist the help of people who already own Jack Russells in finding their ideal dog. Going to Jack Russell trials can also let interested people see a variety of

Every puppy is an individual with his own personality and must be trained and socialized differently.

dogs from all over the country. Trials are listed in the JRTCA's *True Grit* magazine. If you are not set on having a puppy, do not forget that both registries in the US have Jack Russell rescues. The rescue group can often offer a good dog that needs a new home.

PICK OF THE LITTER

The adult personality of the Jack Russell has four major shaping factors: the terrier characteristics, the individual's characteristics, the social interaction during the first four months of life, and the training of the dog.

If two pedigreed dogs are bred, the resulting puppies will vary in quality and personality. Because of the diversity in the breeding of this dog, the variety in a litter is greater than in other breeds. Not all the puppies will be show quality, but not everyone wants a show dog. Most breeders

feel that four months of age is the earliest they can tell the potential of a puppy.

Registration papers will prove that the parents of your puppy were purebred Jack Russell Terriers.

Watching young puppies that are still a part of a litter can tell the prospective owner a lot about the dog's personality. The pup that is aggressively bold is more likely to be dominant. This isn't a problem for the knowledgeable dog owner who can securely establish himself as the leader of the pack, and this particular dog might make the better hunting prospect. The pup who runs up to people and licks their fingers will often be easier to train. The others in the litter will vary from puppies who are outgoing but not assertive to individuals that will always be somewhat shy. Jack Russells that are shy often do not care much for strangers. These make excellent guard dogs and prefer to keep to their primary family of humans. Socializing shy dogs at an early age can help dissipate some of their shyness.

Extremely shy or aggressive animals need homes where the owner is very experienced

The Jack Russell Terrier you choose should be bright-eyed, healthy, alert, and interested in the world around him.

Reputable breeders will screen all Jack Russell Terriers before breeding them to ensure against genetic diseases.

with these challenges. An extremely shy dog will be harder to train and it will take more work to socialize him. If a puppy shows a lot of aggression toward littermates at an early age, this individual may be too aggressive to make a good pet. Shy dogs will sometimes bite out of fear. Overly shy or overly aggressive Jack Russell Terriers should never be bred.

BEFORE TAKING HIM HOME

Make sure when purchasing a puppy that the dog comes with a guarantee. The guarantee should include a health guarantee against some inheritable diseases and a 36-hour guarantee against parvovirus. A veterinarian's examination can detect patellar luxation close to eight weeks of age if this is a concern. Bite problems, as well as pricked ears, will show up between four to six months of age. At the time of purchase, a vet examination similar to what is required for registration at one year of age for the JRTCA is recommended. This will flag some of the dogs that cannot be registered. Before making your final decision, follow these guidelines:

1. Only purchase puppies that are at least eight weeks old. Younger ones are too susceptible to mortality and they haven't had all their lessons from their mom yet.

2. Be sure the puppy has had his shots, including parvo.

3. Be sure to get a bill of sale, the name of the breeder's veterinarian, and the puppy's vaccination record.

4. Find out what kind of food the puppy eats and what kind of feeding schedule the breeder has followed.

5. Get a stud certificate, signed by the owner or other registry for the puppy. Also get at least a four-generation pedigree that has been signed by the breeder.

6. Make sure any guarantees are signed by the breeder and are not just verbal agreements.

REGISTRATION APPLICATIONS

The JRTCA has a unique registration system. Unlike the AKC, a puppy isn't automatically registered when he is born just because the parents were registered. Each dog must apply for registry at one year of age, and the dog must meet breed standards. One year is the age at which the terrier has reached full height and other aspects of maturity, and the dog can be judged on his own merits. Registration applications need to be accompanied by a veterinarian certificate, photos, pedigree, and stud certificate.

The owner of a terrier that is applying for registration must be a current member of the JRTCA. If the terrier is turned down for registration because he did not meet the breed standard or because of a genetic fault, then the terrier is recorded in the club office. The unregisterable terrier is issued a Certificate of Recording. These unregisterable dogs can be shown in all events at JRTCA shows, except for conformation.

PEDIGREES

Unless the potential dog owner has studied blood lines,

Until he is ready to go to his new home, this little pup will need plenty of time with his dam and littermates in order to learn the rules of dogdom.

Your Jack Russell Terrier puppy will soon "grow into" adult food, but until then, stick to the breeders original diet.

pedigrees do little good. With some breeds of dogs where inbreeding is practiced, pedigrees will give a greater indication of what can be expected in the offspring. Because of the JRTCA's rules against inbreeding, there will be a larger amount of diversity in the Jack Russell's characteristics. Pedigrees are far less significant with the Jack Russell than with some other breeds. However, that does not mean that the pedigrees are worthless. Dogs from good breeding stock that have been proven in hunting, showing, and breeding can be traced through their pedigrees. Also, a three- or five-generation pedigree of registered dogs can alert the owner to any problems with certain genetic defects. The best way for the newcomer to understand the significance of certain pedigrees is to ask different breeders their opinion.

Certain kennels are known for producing trial dogs or may have dogs that are a certain size or hair coat. Breeders tend to select for the type of terrier that appeals to them. Some breeders have bred the same dogs often enough to give predictions on what the puppies will be like as adults. Select a breeder that has the desired type of Jack Russell you want and has a good reputation for standing behind the animals he sells.

GROOMING Your Jack Russell Terrier

There are many reasons to groom your Jack Russell on a regular basis. First, grooming is important for the general well being of the dog. It is also important to keep your dog well-groomed if he competes in trials. Regular grooming helps to keep down the accumulation of hair around the house. Maintenance grooming to eliminate shedding will help improve the coat and stimulate the skin of the terrier. While grooming, the owner can also inspect the dog for any nicks or sores and remove any seeds and burrs on the dog.

Establish a grooming routine early in your Jack Russell Terrier's life. Procedures like nail clipping will be far easier with a willing participant.

The Jack Russell Terrier has a double coat consisting of a dense undercoat and a coarse outercoat. The outercoat has a wiry texture to help protect the dog from the elements and from wear and tear when the dog is in the earth. A slicker brush or wire curry comb used for horses is useful for grooming the broken or rough coats. Be sure not to groom too harshly or you will hurt the dog's skin. For smooth coats, a bristle brush helps to remove the excess hair and keeps the dog's coat clean.

Rough coats and broken-coated terriers are stripped either for shows or because the owner finds stripping makes the dog easier to maintain and keep clean. The dead hair is stripped out by using a stripping knife. Hairs are grasped between the thumb and knife and thinned out in the same direction as

Regular grooming is important to the general well being of your Jack Russell Terrier.

40

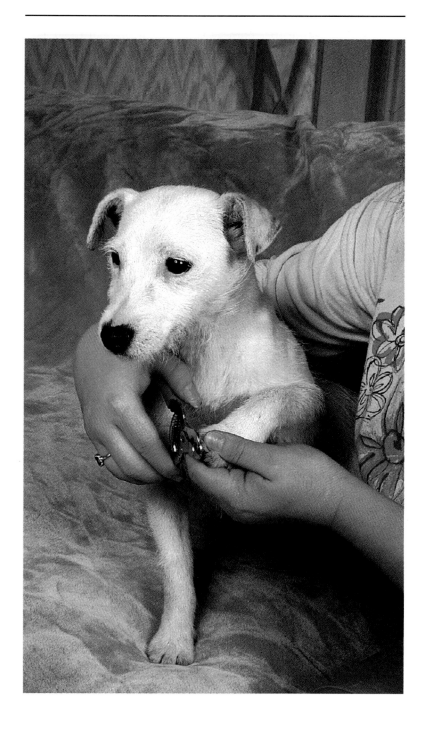

they grow. The dried-out hairs are removed, giving the coat a healthier appearance. For trials, the long hairs are removed until all hairs are of uniform length. Shears are used to trim hairs to the shape of the foot. Trimming and thinning is done to outline the contours of the body. Excess hair is also trimmed off the haunches. The hairs at the tip of the

If you accustom your puppy to regular handling while he is young he will accept grooming far more easily.

tail are removed to better define the tail's shape. Owners only need to strip enough coat to let the terrier be shown at his best. There is no need to remove so much of the coat that the hair is unnaturally smooth. An overgroomed Jack Russell has no place at

shows. Smooth coats need very little grooming for trials and dogs are not bathed for shows. The use of whitener or powders is also discouraged. Such dressing up of a Jack Russell isn't necessary.

Bathing is generally used only to remove foul smells when the dog has rolled in something. Brushing is a better way of removing caked dirt. The Jack Russell's coarse coat is functional and dirt will fall off. If bathing is necessary, be sure to use

a dog shampoo designed for the coarse terrier coat. Before applying the shampoo, wet the dog down with warm water. Work the shampoo into a good lather, then be sure to rinse out all of the shampoo. If all the shampoo isn't removed, it will cause drying or skin irritation. Because these dogs can get cold easily, do not let them outside until they are thoroughly dry.

For Jack Russell Terrier owners who have the privilege of having their dog skunked, there is a homemade recipe that works better than tomato juice. The recipe is as follows: one quart of 3% hydrogen peroxide, 1/4 cup of baking soda, and one teaspoon of liquid soap or dog shampoo.

Mix all of the ingredients in a plastic jug. Put a small amount of triple antibiotic ointment in the dog's eyes before washing and try to avoid getting any soap in his eyes. Do two treatments with the recipe, followed by a thorough water rinse.

The Jack Russell Terrier's coat is functional and dirt will dry and can easily be brushed out. Outback Komet and Ruffian are enjoying a mud bath.

This solution needs to be freshly made each time using new peroxide because peroxide will deteriorate quickly after opening. There are also special shampoos that will remove odors available at pet stores or through mail-order catalogs.

Toenails must be trimmed on a regular basis. This process should be started when the terrier is a puppy and continued throughout the dog's life. Be careful not to cut too close to the quick. If the terrier is hurt, the dog will be more reluctant to hold still for nail trimming the next time. Groomers, veterinarians, and some obedience classes can help teach this task to owners who are uncertain about the procedure. Be sure to keep up on nail maintenance. Nails that are too long can harm the feet or cause improper or uncomfortable gaiting and sometimes grow inward into the sensitive paw.

SHOWING Your Jack Russell Terrier

J ust as Jack Russell Terriers are like no other dog, their shows are like no other dog shows. From the National Trials to local sanctioned trials and fun days, showing a Jack Russell is unique and loaded with fun. Working with Jack Russells always offers delightful surprises, and for the most part, these trials can be a little crazy and provide a lot of entertainment for observers as well as participants. The feeling is relaxed and even at the National Trials, the dress of the exhibitors is casual. While the National Trials are held on a yearly basis, local trials can vary in frequency and location. Although other dog shows seem to orbit around conformation classes, the Jack Russell trials are different as they center around working abilities. Other classes include Racing, Agility, Trailing and Locating, and Obedience. There usually are fun classes that are dictated by the sponsor of the show and your dogs can earn certificates for hunting and agility at trials.

The best way to get the feel of a show is to go to one. Most of the people at the trials are willing to talk about their dogs and the events. Watching also offers great opportunities to learn. These trials are outlined by JRTCA rules, and the show schedule is available through the JRTCA. Trials for the JRTBA club may vary slightly, as will the awards.

CONFORMATION CLASS

This is the class most people see on television. The dogs strut around at the end of a lead or are shown with legs

Although most dog shows center around the conformation class, Jack Russell Terrier shows often emphasize the go-to-ground competition.

stretched out behind and head erect in a trophy-winning pose. In AKC shows, the highest emphasis is placed on the winners of the conformation classes. With Jack Russell Terriers, the highest emphasis is placed on the working classes.

The purpose of a conformation class at a Jack Russell Terrier show is to display breeding stock.

The purpose of a conformation class is to display breeding stock. Judges weigh their opinion by awarding ribbons to the dog they feel comes closest to the ideal Jack Russell Terrier. Dogs are led loosely on leads while correctness of gait is judged, which concerns how straight the dog's legs are and how naturally the dog moves. The dog's chest size and other conformational structure is checked. Because no dog is perfect, the final decision of one judge may not be the same as another.

Some basic training is necessary in order for owners to show their dog. For example, if the owner holds the lead tightly, then the dog cannot move naturally and may appear to have a bad gait or an upright shoulder. Terriers exhibited in conformation classes need to be neat and clean, but not overly groomed. If the terrier has a rough coat, it will probably need to be stripped. This is best done four to six weeks ahead of show time and is explained in the grooming chapter. At all JRTCA trials, conformation champions for working terrier classes require a working certificate.

At a Jack Russell show, the judge picks a dog that looks like he is ready to go hunting. To compete, the Jack Russell needs to be in fit condition. The dogs must also be trained to let the judges handle them. Judges often want to measure the dog's girth by putting their hands around the dog's rib cage. This is not a good time for the dog to snap at someone, so the Jack Russell must be accustomed to having strangers handle him.

Ring etiquette is expected when showing in conformation classes. Exhibitors are expected not to talk to the judge while he is judging the class, even if they know the judge personally.

Exhibitors should only ask for a critique of their terrier after the judge has finished for the day. Good sportsmanship is always a must.

Conformation classes are a reflection of an educated judge's opinion. The best way to evaluate a dog for conformation is to see how the dog has been placed by several judges, not just one. Do not criticize the competition and/or the judge; accept the dog's placement with a smile. Remember, these trials are supposed to be fun.

GO-TO-GROUND

Go-To-Ground is an event that lets the dogs go through manmade tunnels to locate two caged rats. A series of wooden liners that simulate an underground den is created. At the end of this curved and twisted path, the quarry waits. The cage of rats is protected and they are never hurt. The dogs are graded on time they take to complete the course and how they work the quarry. Participants don't need a lot of preparation for showing in this event because

This is a picture of a Go-To-Ground course. The flags help to keep track of the dog's progress.

the novice and pre-novice classes are designed for the beginners. Puppies from four to six months of age go-to-ground in the pre-novice class, and the judges show the owners what to do. The novice class is for older puppies or adults that are competing in this event for the first time. Once the dog has succeeded at this class, he is entered into the open class. For the Go-To-Ground classes, the dog has one minute to reach the quarry and may leave and re-enter the tunnel several times. The dog is expected to work the quarry for 30 seconds.

This agility obstacle simulates an underground tunnel.

AGILITY

Think of all the stunts that dogs do in the movies, and gather all the props and put them inside a fenced area. That's a Jack Russell agility class. Agility consists of an obstacle course and is one of the most popular events for exhibitors. Because this is a sanctioned event at JRTCA, classes are entered for awards. In addition, an agility certificate can be earned. There are three categories for agility certificates: an On-Lead Certificate, and Agility I and II Off-Lead certificates. A certificate for Advanced On-Lead is being developed. On-lead certificates consist of a combination of novice and advanced qualifying scores. For Agility I and II Off-Lead, a dog must earn three legs in each division under two different judges.

For the basic novice and advanced On-Lead and Agility I courses, the obstacles include bar jumps, a tire jump, a dog walk, a see-saw, an A-frame structure, a collapsed tunnel, a closed tunnel, and a pause table. The Agility II course is more challenging. Added to the previously mentioned obstacles are a crawl tunnel, weave poles, and a pause box. The hoop tunnel, sway bridge, see-sawing plank, and platform jump are optional.

Rules for the course include: All courses must be fenced, no touching of the dog, no dogs under one year of age, either the dog is entered in On-Lead or Off-Lead, but not both, and if the dog decides to answer the call of nature while competing, he will be disqualified.

Agility is an exciting sport that tests a dog's coordination. This Jack Russell Terrier takes a jump with ease.

At the Nationals, child/junior agility on-lead is offered to participants ages 6 through 14. Another class at the Nationals that generates a lot of fun is the Strip Pairs Relay. For this class, on-lead and off-lead agility has the added dimension of switching the dog controller.

RACING

This is perhaps the most popular of all the classes for spectators at a Jack Russell Terrier trial. Terriers are placed in individual starting boxes. Their excitement practically vibrates in the air as the dogs wait for the starting gate to open. A tuft of fur that is attached to a wire and rapidly pulled along by a motor is followed closely by the little terriers. Nothing will stop these dogs from getting that little tuft as they run at top speed, sometimes leaping over small jumps. Well, almost nothing stops the terriers. Sometimes a dog stops after a short distance and tries to paw off the muzzle that is required for racing. This is why smart competitors get dogs accustomed to the muzzle long before show time. All kinds of antics occur in this event. Sometimes novice dogs lose interest part way and stop to look around for their owner. One dog jumped the fence during a race and went into the tunnel at the nearby Go-To-Ground course. On the television show *America's Home Videos,* one dog competing in this race was caught on tape when he stopped in front of the hay bales and lifted his leg to relieve himself.

And they're off! Jack Russell Terriers love flat racing; nothing can keep them from chasing the lure!

At the end of the race course are a stack of hay bales with a small hole. The winner is the first dog through the hole. Dogs have been known to jump up and over the hay bales, which disqualifies them, instead of going through the hole.

Jack Russell Terriers usually get the gist of racing pretty quickly, so practice at home isn't as critical as with agility training. The terriers start racing at four months of age and older. Racing includes a variety from flat races, steeplechase races, and stake races. Stake races offer donated purses that can be as high as $200.00.

OBEDIENCE

There are six categories of this class offered at the Nationals. Sanctioned and fun trials can vary. The utility obedience class deals with a signal exercise, scent discrimination, directed retrieve, moving, stand and examinations, and directed jumping. Open obedience is judged individually on heel free, figure 8, drop on recall, retrieve on flat, and retrieve over high jump or broad jump. The three-minute-long sit and a five-minute-long down can be judged as a group. Novice obedience is also judged individually on heel on leash, figure 8, stand for exam, heel off leash, and recall off leash. The one-minute sit/stay and a three-minute down/stay are judged as a group in this class. A brace is where two dogs are performing subnovice exercises together. The dogs are judged on subnovice criteria. Dogs may be on two leads or coupled on one. Braces are to be judged on precision. For this class, the brace that works as one stands the best chance of winning. Junior handlers have their own class that is judged as subnovice.

Trailing and Locating

This event is open to any adult Jack Russell. The terriers first travel through a short liner, then they follow a scent that is laid down on a path through an open area. This event is designed to simulate locating quarry above ground. The dog is worked off lead and is expected to complete the course in three minutes. Points are awarded on accuracy and time. At the Nationals, proceeds from this event are used to benefit the JRTCA Humane Services Project.

Trials, Local Fun Days, and the Nationals

Local fun days offer many of the standard events but are not sanctioned or competitive. These are usually attended by local terrier owners who are looking for an opportunity to practice with their dogs and can offer unique events of the sponsor's design. These trials usually have lower fees than sanctioned trials.

Sanctioned trials must follow JRTCA rules and are competitions between dogs. These are often attended by

people who have traveled from all over the United States. Judges are either JRTCA

"Bertha" and her owner Will Hahn practice a timed sit for an agility competition.

Local fun days can be wonderful experiences for terrier owners and enthusiasts, as well as for Jack Russell Terriers themselves.

certified or flown in from England and have met the JRTCA criteria. If a JRTCA judge is present, then agility awards and hunting awards can be worked on. Unlike other dog shows, there is no point system at sanctioned trials. The awards given a dog are just the ribbons for that particular trial and are not accumulative.

The National Trial is the big annual JRTCA dog show. This show draws people from all over the world. In comparison to the sanctioned local trials, the National has a lot of entries per class, which can range from 30 to 50 or more. Any dog who lands a ribbon in any of these classes has received a great honor.

In general, trials for Jack Russells are different from other breed shows. The lack of accumulative point systems keeps down the politics that plague other shows in which winning has greater gains. The local trials are usually run through the efforts of volunteers. The atmosphere, even at the Nationals, is social. These are great places to meet Jack Russell people, share information, and have a good time.

WORKING Jack Russell Terriers

Jack Russell Terrier stays true to his original heritage and his roots are in hunting. They were first bred in England when fox hunting was popular. Hounds, horses, and terriers (including the Jack Russell) were employed to help get rid of the unwanted fox and offer excitement to those who could afford the sport. Horses and hounds would pound across the field in pursuit of a fox. If the fox dove into a hole to hide, the terrier men were summoned. Jack Russells were used to locate the fox, go down into the hole, tunnel or den, and flush out the quarry. If the Jack Russell couldn't flush out the fox, the terrier men helped by digging to the hole. Sometimes the Jack Russell was killed by the prey. Occasionally the dog died in the tunnel because the tunnel collapsed or the dog couldn't be dug out of the hole and suffocated. In those times, losing Jack Russells was to be expected.

Today in England, people still go fox hunting on horseback and they still take their Jack Russell Terriers. To hunt, most people join a hunt club. Fox hunting in England has become an expensive sport that people now participate in not to kill foxes, but to have a good time riding and chasing the fox across the countryside. Although the Jack Russell Terriers still go along to flush the fox out of the hole, ironically enough, the foxes aren't supposed to be in the holes to begin with. The night before the hunt, the terrier men go out and cover all of the fox holes. Early in the morning, they go out again and make sure the fox holes are still covered. Invariably, the fox finds somewhere to hole up, and the terriers are summoned.

The role of the Jack Russell Terriers in the hunt in the United States is different. The prey in America varies from woodchuck to groundhog to fox, and even to rats. The dog as a whole still has maintained the brains and good conformation that hunting demands. In the pitch dark of a tunnel, these dogs make decisions in life-threatening situations. No two dogs work alike. People who hunt with dogs say they do so because when the dog is hunting, the enthusiasm the dog has doing his work is not only rewarding to the dog, but to the owner as well. A lot of hunting with Jack Russells is done as a sport in which the prey is found and then released to chase another day.

Hunting with a Jack Russell follows guidelines designed to help protect the dog. One thing that is never hunted is skunks. Unfortunately, sometimes this happens accidentally. The dog cannot flush the skunk from its hole, because the skunk will spray in defense. The spray becomes concentrated in a small enclosed area and is toxic. If a Jack Russell is ever sprayed underground, immediate medical attention is necessary to save the dog's life. The dog must be dug out and rushed to a veterinarian, where steroids can help to keep the dog out of shock and prevent more permanent damage that can lead to death.

It is imperative that a Jack Russell Terrier never be allowed to enter a hole in which he cannot be dug out. These enthusiastic hunters have been known to stay with live prey for days and need to be rescued!

Any ground that a Jack Russell is sent into must be a hole in which the dog can be dug out. Some Jack Russells have been known to stay with live prey for days without food and water. To rescue the dog, he must be dug out. Some holes are hard, if not impossible, to dig. You cannot dig through rock very well, and if the hole is also in a bank, then the height of the bank is added to how deep you must dig to retrieve a dog. All dogs sent down holes need to wear electronic locator collars.

A second terrier is rarely sent in behind the first because this may push the first dog into a dangerous situation. When hunting, the dogs are in an excited state, and the second dog may bite the first dog. The first dog may be pushed into prey that will attack the dog in self defense. Hunters do not expect their terrier to locate, enter the hole, and work the quarry the first time they ever go hunting. Some Jack Russells are automatic workers, but most need time to develop their skills. The owner also needs time to learn their dog's strong points and abilities.

The age at which a Jack Russell Terrier becomes interested in hunting varies greatly with each individual.

Hunting age varies with the individual dog's personality. Even in the same litter, one dog may start working at seven months of age by baying at a hole. His littermate may not care about entering a hole until he is 14 months old, and some dogs do not hunt well until they are three years of age. Different dogs need different amounts of time to become mentally ready. Owners are also cautious with younger dogs because they do not have their adult teeth. They will not send the youngster into a hole when the dog can come up against dangerous quarry that has its adult teeth. Also, a young dog that is not ready to hunt could be mentally damaged by a bad experience.

CHOOSING TO HUNT

Some Jack Russell owners do not plan on hunting with their dog when they buy him, but decide to hunt after they start a breeding program. Because the Jack Russell Terrier is a working dog and hunting certificates can be earned, hunting with the Jack Russell can become a natural step for an active breeder. What appeals to some about hunting, compared to other activities they can participate in with their dogs, is that the dog so thoroughly enjoys hunting. Although racing is often a favorite event for this type of dog, trials usually mean the dog will be confined to small areas where the dog must endure waiting and other dogs that are incessantly barking. Hunting is usually done out in the countryside, where the air isn't scented with automobile fumes. The noises are low, most coming from the wild animals or breezes in the trees. Hunting offers good times and good experiences for people who like the outdoors.

Many Jack Russell Terriers and their owners enjoy hunting because it allows them to have good times outdoors in the quiet countryside.

Some people may be bothered by the idea of killing animals. Many Jack Russell owners who hunt practice the hunt and release method. Others who do kill the animals do so to help restore the balance of nature that people have upset by limiting the areas where wildlife can live. People have already destroyed the natural predator-prey relationship. Wise hunters can help re-establish the balance of nature and conserve it. When nature is out of balance, the animals grow in population and often face

a cruel death by starvation in the winter time. Also, hunting rodents, such as rats that are infesting a barn, can eliminate the need for biohazardous poisons.

Hunting with the Jack Russell changes the relationship between the terrier and his owner. People who hunt with their dogs have reported that there is not only a resulting bond between themselves and the dog, but there is also a dramatic change in a dog that hunts for the first time. It's like a light goes on. The dog suddenly becomes more responsive to his owner, and the dog that has been immature seems to mature overnight.

People who decide to try hunting with their terrier need to check with state and wildlife officials to see what kind of animal can legally be hunted and what the rules are about disturbing dens. Things that an owner needs to arm himself with for hunting include a locator collar, a shovel, a steel bar, and a flashlight. This is the minimum amount of equipment you will need to take into the field. More equipment can be kept in the vehicle. It is recommended that you learn to locate the dog without the collar, in case the collar slips off in a hole. The steel bar helps with finding which direction the tunnel follows after the entrance. Sometimes if the tunnel is shallow, the dog can be felt underneath the surface of the ground by resting your hands on the dirt. The dogs can also be heard moving and scratching beneath the ground.

Jack Russell Terriers enjoy hunting so much you should not be surprised if they go-to-ground anywhere—even in your bedroom!

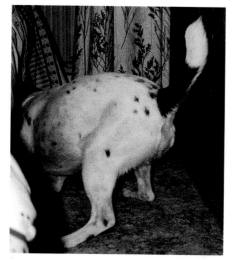

Your Jack Russell Terrier needs to be in good physical working condition for hunting. Just like people, a dog cannot go out and work the whole day when he is just used to walking a little. This is a sport for the dog that is totally fit. Even dogs in shape will wear themselves out on the adventure, needing a few days to rest afterwards.

You need to prepare your dog for hunting by making certain he is current with his inoculations. Rabies is the most important shot. If hunting in an area where plague has ever been reported, spray the dog with flea spray both before and after the hunt. If plague is an active problem in a particular area, don't hunt there. Although the dog cannot get sick from plague infested fleas, the owner can. Other problems a hunting dog can encounter include

It is important to safeguard your dog's health if you plan to allow him to hunt. Be sure that his vaccinations are kept up to date and he is in good physical condition before any jaunt in the great outdoors.

snake bites, skunks, porcupines, and coon paralysis. Coon paralysis is caused by a virus that is transmitted by a raccoon and dogs afflicted with this suffer nerve paralysis.

Whether the owner of a Jack Russell Terrier wants to or not, the dog definitely will want to hunt. If the dog isn't on a leash while walking across a field, he may take off in hot pursuit of a rabbit, prairie dog, or domestic cat. Dogs have disappeared down holes even though their owners were trying to call them back. Sometimes the dog reappears after a while, other times the owner may have to wait until the terrier comes up for air to nab him. Once in a while, the owner has to dig the dog out. These dogs each have been bred to work the prey differently. A soft dog will bay at the quarry, a hard dog will attack. Some, in rare instances, will just locate the hole.

A MAN AND HIS DOG

Ken Chambers lives near Lexington, Kentucky, along with lots of groundhogs. In the midst of horse country, pastures full of groundhogs can be dangerous to horses. The holes made by

Ken Chambers and his Jack Russell Terriers are famous for their varmint control techniques in Kentucky.

groundhogs can cause a horse to break a leg and have to be destroyed. When people in the area have problems, they call Ken. He and his Jack Russell Terriers offer their services free of charge.

Ken takes his terriers to the pasture or field that is infested. A terrier goes into one of the holes and tries to get the animal to bolt. Ken also takes along another dog called a Lurcher (a large dog often a cross of a Greyhound and a Border Collie). The Lurcher catches the groundhogs that are flushed from the hole. Sometimes the groundhog will not come out. If it doesn't, and Ken cannot call his dog out, then he uses his electronic collar to locate the dog. Once the dog is located, he digs him out. He may come back another day to try to flush the groundhog from the hole.

Ken has 15 Jack Russell Terriers and he and his dogs have hunted all kinds of game. Ken is the owner of Windermere Solo, who was the stud dog of the year in the 1994 National finals. Ken owns five dogs that are "Medallion Dogs." A Medallion Dog is the highest honor for hunting in the field, and involves the terrier getting natural hunting certificates for three different prey.

Ken keeps his dogs kenneled, but never keeps more than a bitch and male together. If the dogs are not supervised, they will get into squabbles that can turn deadly. Ken also does a lot of judging for Go-To-Ground events that are described in detail in the trial section of this book.

Ken's motto is to breed for and to protect the hunting aspect of this terrier and strives to breed his dogs for a height between 10 and 12 ¹/₂ inches.

In order to earn the Natural Hunting Certificate Below Ground in the Field, the dog and owner must work together to unearth the quarry.

WORKING CERTIFICATES

The JRTCA gives out three types of certificates for working: the Natural Hunting Certificate Below Ground in the Field, the Sporting Certificate, and the Trial Certificate.

The Natural Hunting Certificate Below Ground in the Field is the highest certificate awarded. This certificate is awarded only to registered dogs. The dog and owner work together, and the dog must prove his ability for the specific quarry below ground. Different quarry allows for different certificates. When three Natural Hunting Certificates are received by a terrier and his owner, the JRTCA Bronze Working Terrier Medallion for Special Merit in the Field is awarded.

The Sporting Certificate is awarded to Jack Russells who have worked successfully to nonformidable or above-ground quarry such as squirrels and rats.

The Trial Certificate is awarded to Jack Russells with an 100% score in the Open Class of the Go-To-Ground Division at a JRTCA-sanctioned trial.

TRAINING Your Jack Russell Terrier

Experience is what you get just after you need it.

The most important thing to do before you begin training your puppy is to educate yourself with training books or videos, advice from owners, and puppy and dog training classes. You need to start teaching your puppy early. For the first year you will need a lot of patience, and you'll need to be consistent with your training. If you hang in there, you'll have a great dog as a final reward.

Don't spend too much time on repetitive training and don't forget that this is only a puppy. A puppy's attention span for learning is shorter than it will be as an adult. Break up training sessions into short lessons throughout the day. Attention span is something that can be lengthened slowly. Finally, if you teach your dog nothing else, you must teach him to come to you when called.

If you are patient and consistent when training your puppy, you'll have a great dog as a final reward.

If you find that there are training challenges that you can't figure out, seek professional help. Even if the owner needs no help training the dog, an obedience class can help the dog with the socialization process and help the owner train the dog to pay attention to him or her in a distracting situation. Be sure

the dog trainer has experience with Jack Russell Terriers. Help is also available on the Internet. The JRTCA offers free advice to people who log on to their web site.

Although your puppy wants to learn what you have to teach him, keep in mind that his attention span is short and he will need plenty of repetition and praise.

JACK RUSSELL TRAINING STRATEGIES

Start With a Good Foundation

The key to living happily with a Jack Russell Terrier is training, and training has four building blocks: Bonding, Establishing Yourself as Leader of the Pack, Rewards, and Discipline.

The four building blocks of training are intertwined. For instance, discipline deals with never letting the dog get the upper hand. The dog must see you as the leader of the pack. This does not mean the dog needs to be beaten for misbehavior. Beating a Jack Russell Terrier never creates a well-behaved dog. With this sensitive breed, it destroys them. Rewards and bonding also play into obedience. When you see any of the Jack Russells perform on television, you can bet the tricks they are doing were trained for with rewards, not punishment. Rewards such as praise strengthen the bond between owner and dog.

Bonding with the dog is so important that the dog used for Eddie on the television show *Frasier* lives with his current trainer. Professional

Successful training relies on your ability to effectively establish yourself as the "leader of the pack" while maintaining a close relationship with your dog.

Bonding is by far one of the most important building blocks of training. Allowing your Jack Russell to sleep by your side will help foster his feelings of trust in you.

trainers have learned the advantage of working with a dog that is bonded to them and respects them. Respect again goes back to the dog seeing the owner as leader of the pack.

BONDING

Bonding deals with winning over your Jack Russell Terrier's heart.

There are several ways to bond with your Jack Russell, and most of these techniques work with dogs of all ages.

Sleep with Your Jack Russell Terrier

Owners may not want to do this until the puppy is housebroken, and some people do not ever want a dog in their bed at night. It is fine, however, if you are sitting around watching television, to set the dog or puppy on your lap or

The intelligent and energetic Jack Russell Terrier is an adept and able pupil when trained properly.

next to you instead of putting him in his crate to sleep. A few strokes while the dog nods off does not hurt either. You can even get the dog in the habit of sleeping by your feet.

Hand Feeding

One path to the Jack Russell's heart is through his stomach. Feeding the puppy or dog by hand does a lot for bonding. Also, in a pack, the leader controls the food. When you feed by hand, the dog realizes you have complete control over the food and you are the leader. When you put food in a bowl and walk off, the dog chooses when and how much to eat.

Feeding by hand does not mean you have to have a fat Jack Russell. You can feed the normal ration of puppy or dog food and do not have to use any extra treats. This only needs to be done for a short time and reinforced occasionally.

Exercise

Exercising a Jack Russell Terrier helps form a strong bond. This does not mean turning the dog out in the backyard. Grab a leash and go for a run or long walk. This is best done alone, with just the owner and the Jack Russell. No other dogs or people should come along. Take the dog to a park and let him smell some new smells and see new sights. Exercising increases bonding and gives you status as leader of the pack because you are taking the dog somewhere, or leading him, like the pack leader would.

To aid in the socialization process, take your dog with you on outings. Your Jack Russell Terrier will love going places with you and will enjoy the activity.

Another way to form strong bonds is to take the dog along with you when you go places. Take him in the car to the store. If it is a store where dogs are tolerated, take the dog in with you. Take the dog to a horse show. Of course, be sure to leash the dog. These dogs like activity, and they will grow to love their owners if they get to go places with them, just like you become closer to friends you spend time with. Hunting is also an event that forms a strong bond.

Establish Yourself as Leader of the Pack

Dogs need to know who is in charge. Humans must never be anywhere below the dog in the hierarchy of the pack. Dominance goes back to the pack nature of a dog. The pack has a definite order of seniority. There is always a leader of the dog pack. All the other individuals get privileges according to where they fall in the order of hierarchy. Just because the Jack Russell owner is paying the bills, does not for a moment in the Jack Russell's mind make the human the leader of the pack.

Dogs look up to the leader of the pack like their owners look up to sport heroes and movie stars, but interaction with the leader of the pack is different. The leader of the pack gets first choice of food, sleeping arrangements, and mates. The leader of the pack will also hand out discipline. When the human takes the necessary place as leader of the pack, he or she needs to be sure they do not compromise on any of these issues with the dog. First the owner needs to control the food. Feeding by hand, as mentioned earlier, is a good start.

Dog aggression is used to establish who is dominant in the pack. This varies within all breeds and when expressed in hunting, is not a fault for a Jack Russell, unless it is excessive. The reason dominance varies in any breed is to help keep pack order. Different dogs have different hierarchical standings—not all in the pack can be the boss. This allows for most dogs to readily accept the human as their boss if the human asserts himself effectively.

Exercising and activity will help direct your Jack Russell Terrier's energy towards positive goals. It's good for humans, too!

The dog shows aggression related to dominance by growling and showing teeth. In the pack, aggressiveness to establish dominance rarely gets bloody. This isn't usually meant to be a fight to the death. Dogs more often engage in a growl, show of teeth, and sometimes a quick snap. Another way a dog shows dominance is to place his muzzle over the back of the subordinate dog, or stand over the dog. Occasionally a dog will grab another by the scruff of the neck and shake. Since this is the type of language the dog understands, people can use similar techniques to communicate to their dogs.

A good rule to keep in mind about dominance is that it is not misbehavior, but misbehavior can result from an unresolved dominance issue. The rule of thumb for a dominant dog is that whenever possible, move up in the pecking order of the pack. The dominance issue is not just an issue for the male dogs. Females in this breed can show more aggression than males.

At about 10 weeks of age is when the first dominant and subordinate behavior is shown in a puppy. From three to six months, the owner needs to assert his position as leader.

Often, the first time an owner sees a display of dominance is at the food bowl. When the dog is eating and a family member approaches the dish, they may get growled at. This is a good time to put the pup in his place. Take away the food. Let him know who is in charge. Asserting oneself with a dog doesn't mean getting bit. Using gloves and a jacket can give the owner an advantage of protection of the hands and arms. Even if the dog's attempt to snap a hand doesn't hurt, be sure to discipline the dog.

Jack Russell owners will find challenges to their dominance in the owner's bed. When a Jack Russell Terrier takes over your bed by growling at you, you can bet the owner's position as leader of the pack is being challenged. The owner must assert himself as boss. Move the dog to the floor, use gloves if you are afraid of getting bit, and discipline the dog if he snaps or tries to bite. Remember the leader of the pack hands out the discipline and keeps the subordinates in their place. The Jack Russell Terrier must never feel he is the leader of the pack.

Little actions mean a lot to dogs. The dog keeps score even the if owner is not noticing or doesn't think the issue matters. One example is if the owner steps around a dog who is in the way. Normally it does not matter if an owner steps around a dog laying in his path, but the dominant dog will chalk this up as a victory in the dominance war. If this is a problem, you need to call out the command "move." If the dog still does not respond, physically move him out of your way. One important rule with dominance is do not try and out-muscle the dog. Threats come across as challenges, and so does abuse. The dedicated dominant dog will fight when challenged.

Although he may look harmless, this Jack Russell Terrier puppy will need discipline and guidance to become a valued family member.

Six or seven months of age in a young dog's life is the second time dominance becomes an issue. This time the behavior is fueled by hormones. This is the dreaded teenager Jack Russell. A good technique for keeping the dog in his place in the pack is to teach the dog to sit and wait while his food dish is being put down. The dog must wait until the owner gives the okay to eat before leaving the sitting position. This gives the dog the

A pup's personality will be evident in the way he interacts with his littermates. These two compete for "top dog."

message that not only does the owner control the food, but the dog will have to wait to get it. In working through dominance issues, the owner needs a lot of determination and consistency in discipline.

Half the torture of the dominance issue can be

Puppy obedience classes will not only help both you and your Jack Russell Terrier master proper training exercises, they will also allow your puppy time to socialize with other dogs.

eliminated by spaying or neutering. The closer the dog is to five months old, the better effect this action will have. Spaying and neutering older dogs does not have the same effect, because even though the hormonal stimulus is removed, the dog has already learned the behavior.

With some dogs, after about a year, the dominance issue is settled. Other Jack Russells may have to be reminded again and again. As mentioned before, using the dog's natural language is a good way to discipline with a dominance issue. Dogs will grab a subordinate by the scruff of the neck and sometimes shake. Owners can assert dominance the same way by grabbing the scruff of the dog or grabbing both sides of the neck and shaking. Do not hesitate to hold the dog down or pin him until he quits growling.

The Jack Russell is a spirited and energetic dog who will want to have his say in most things, like this game of tug-of-war.

DOMINANCE AND ASSERTIVENESS

Sometimes a Jack Russell Terrier that is asserting himself is difficult to distinguish from one that is acting dominant. By definition, assertiveness is defined as the tendency for the dog to maintain or defend his rights and express himself forcefully or boldly. Dominance is defined as when the dog shows aggression, or when the dog is inclined to move or act in a hostile fashion. Deciding if your Jack Russell is being dominant or assertive can be difficult, because sometimes they're being a little of both.

This attentive Jack Russell is probably awaiting his next command. Do not correct your Jack Russell too often—with this dog's ego, overlooking an error is usually best.

Some actions engaged by the Jack Russell are not part of a dominance issue. By nature this dog will want to have an equal say in things such as where he sleeps, how much attention he gets, when to go in and out of the house, and when to play. If he can manage, he will try and train the owner on all of these issues.

The assertive dog can learn quickly, and has no problems with the fact that humans are the leaders of the pack, but the assertive Jack Russell is still inclined to express his opinion. Owners can show the dog something once during the training session and when the task is done correctly, the dog expects to be rewarded and left alone. Repetition for no reason is not up this dog's alley. Immediately repeating the trick several times invites the dog to find a way to do the trick differently. What is worse, the dog will often ask why he should do this trick. Trainers of "star" dogs are quick to be sure they don't overtrain for a part. A lot of praise with a bonded dog works well when training the Jack Russell. Owners must take care not to rub it in when the dog makes a mistake. With this dog's ego, overlooking an error is best. Correct when the dog doesn't understand what's wanted and punish only when undisputed defiance is seen.

REWARDS

Treats

Positive reinforcement is enough to make most Jack Russells happy to obey any command.

Years ago a scientist named Pavlov used a variety of stimuli to get dogs to drool saliva. Basically what he discovered was that the best way to administer rewards was intermittently. At first the owner may give a treat every time the dog does something correctly, but soon you can wean the dog off constant treats. Start substituting the treat with a pat and lavish praise, saving the treat for periodical reinforcement. This is what a true treat is—something that is occasionally given. Never knowing when that treat is available is a great reinforcer.

When using treats to train, an empty stomach goes further than a full one. Also, the Jack Russell owner must be careful or the dog will quickly learn how to barter for treats. A good reward to give your dog is praise.

Praise

Most people get too serious when they train and do not praise their dog enough. The best and fastest way to train a puppy is to play with him. When the puppy just starts to do something right, get really excited and happy. Praise the dog verbally such as "Good Boy!!! Oh look what a good boy you are, you're the best ever!!!" Use a playful and excited tone of voice. Make your praise sound as if you and your dog are having the best time of your life. Jump up and down, pat your legs, and act like a fool. Dogs love it when you act like a fool for them. They start to pay attention to you, like maybe you could be more fun than that squeaky toy. When you get your dog excited, the dog will want to do what you want him to do. The dog figures

Using play and praise is the best and fastest way to train a Jack Russell Terrier.

Your Jack Russell Terrier is sure to get into plenty of mischief as a puppy. Remember that although discipline is important, the punishment should always fit the crime.

that maybe you are as interesting as those new smells and just maybe worth paying attention to, just to see what you'll do next. Once you've got his attention, you can start toning it down a little and get to work.

DISCIPLINE

Punishment is meant to correct bad behavior. Beating a dog is uncalled for no matter how severe the offense, although a light swat may help get a point across. But before the owner raises his hand to his Jack Russell Terrier, it is important to understand when and why a swat might do the trick.

A general rule about punishment is that what works for one dog may not work for another. This breed is sensitive and abuse will destroy his character. Some good kinds of discipline include liberal scolding, a light swat, a scruff hold, and scolding with time in isolation in another room. Remember, never use a crate for punishment.

When administering discipline, remember the crime should fit the punishment and the offender. You must get through and get a response, or the punishment is no good. Sometimes a spray of water after telling a dog to quit barking is effective. Some dogs are not phased by this. For some dogs, a harsh word will make him cower. This varies with each dog's personality. If a dog is snapping, a well-aimed slap across the mouth with a stern "no" can get the point across. The swat is meant to startle the dog and frighten him more than punish. It can get the dog's attention. A second swat once the dog stops is not necessary. Punishment also needs to fit the frequency of the misbehavior. For example, continual scratching on the refrigerator brings firmer punishment, and the punishment must fit the temperament of the wrongdoer.

A young puppy will not know the difference between good and bad behavior. It is up to you, the owner, to teach him what is acceptable in your household.

When punishing, use the "leader of the pack" rules established by wild dogs and wolves. The punishment is quick and to the point, combined with angry noises. Your tone of voice should mimic growling. The punishment is meant to intimidate. The best way to punish the Jack Russell is to scare him. Some people do this by slapping a whip on the ground or using a can of coins shaken close to the dog. Picking the dog up by the scruff can also get the point across. This is a powerless position that can be humiliating to the dog's big ego.

Ideally, instant punishment is the best. Punish at the time of the crime. However this isn't always possible. If something is found chewed up, use the evidence when disciplining. Never discipline without evidence there. The owner needs to bring the dog to the evidence, then react to it, not drag the dog yelling to the site. Also, never use your temper to punish. The idea is to communicate to the dog, not get revenge.

Always start punishment at low levels and work your way up. Start with sharp words. If that doesn't bring a corrective response, then start climbing the ladder of discipline. Make the reprimand more harsh. Never start with the most severe discipline. Jack Russells vary in sensitivity, but some are extremely sensitive. Shy dogs must have less harsh correction or time in confinement rather than physical punishment or too much yelling. The shy dog will quickly become timid if the punishment is excessive. Be sure to watch the dog's reaction while punishing. Also, remember that during adolescence, the dog will be at his all-time worst, just as with all teenagers. Patience and a sense of humor will help the owner survive.

A tap on the paw is appropriate with the word "no." If that doesn't work, a slap is fine, and a firmer "no." Sometimes a tap under the jaw is enough. If the dog is trying to kill the cat, then the punishment needs to be the most severe. Also, dogs must be firmly disciplined when they kill chickens or chase

Jack Russell Terriers must be properly socialized and carefully supervised if they are to live peacefully among other pets.

Remember that Jack Russell Terriers are hunting dogs and will chase after animals they view as prey. In order to correct this, immediate discipline is necessary.

livestock. The dog's life may be at stake. People can legally shoot dogs that are chasing their livestock.

Of course, there's always the individual who ignores punishment. For the defiant dog who is not impressed by moderate punishment, the owner must find something that is noticeable to the dog. These dogs endure the blows then walk off totally self-righteous. What may be more effective is tying the dog in a corner for about 10-30 minutes. Another possibility is throwing a glass of water on the dog. The owner of this type of dog needs to figure out what gets to the dog.

Dogs are not machines. They make mistakes. Do not punish every error. Obedience deals with correcting the dog and disciplining misbehavior. Be sure the dog is being defiant before punishing. Although dogs are not given credit for certain emotions, a Jack Russell seems to get embarrassed about some of his mistakes. If the owner feels the dog realizes his mistake, then the error is fine to overlook. Owners need to learn to read their dogs like they would a friend. Remember, the Jack Russell likes to please and will not want his owner to be extremely displeased. But beware, until this dog is well trained, he can be quick to take advantage of lenient owners.

MAKING TRAINING EASIER

The biggest part of training is figuring out how to make your Jack Russell want to do what you want him to do. And the best way to do that is through communication, play, and praise.

Energy Reduction

A couple of things need to be taken care of before an owner can effectively train a Jack Russell. One is the energy level of the dog. Owners will think the little mass of dog is moving at the speed of light instead of paying attention if the dog's energy level isn't worked off before training. A short walk or play time before training helps the dog relax.

When training a Jack Russell, keep up the variety and do not plug away at the same lessons every day. Lessons only need to be repeated every few days. Drilling is not the key to training Jack Russells, insistence is. The owner must insist on obedience. For instance, if the dog has just been told to sit and doesn't, push his bottom down and praise and pet the dog as if he had obeyed the verbal command. Don't ever think that putting off dealing with behavioral problems makes them go away. And don't forget that dogs in general learn in spurts, and may do some backsliding.

Training your Jack Russell Terrier will be much more successful if you allow him time to play and expend some energy beforehand.

COMMUNICATION

Eye contact is a key factor when communicating with the Jack Russell Terrier. The Jack Russell Terrier will look at his owner when he wants something or is trying to communicate. The problem with the "look" can be twofold: First, the owner may not be tuned in to notice, and second, the puppy or dog may be looking right at you as if he just said something crystal clear, but the

Jack Russell Terriers are intelligent and inquisitive and will investigate anything in their path.

Eye contact is a key factor in successful communication with your Jack Russell Terrier.

owner probably won't know what the dog means. An owner needs to be aware of the dog's direct look and learn to interpret what is being communicated by his dog.

Some Jack Russells that are trying to tune out their owner's requests will do so by avoiding eye contact. You must work to eliminate excuses for the dog not to look at you. Just like with a child, you need to know you have your dog's full attention. Speak the dog's name. If the dog doesn't look directly at you, touch the nose of the Jack Russell with a finger. If the dog doesn't follow the finger to the owner's eyes, the owner can hold the muzzle and position the dog's head, forcing eye contact. This needs to be brief at first. The amount of time needed to work up to longer periods of eye

The athletic and agile Jack Russell Terrier loves to perform for an audience— especially for a reward!

contact depends upon the dog. The more stubborn dogs will resist looking at the owner at all, but this exercise will help break through the stubborn streak. By practicing eye contact, the owner will notice an improvement in his or her relationship with the dog. The dog's manners and behavior will improve. Eye contact exercises are best done in an isolated area, free of distractions, other people, and other dogs or pets.

The Jack Russell Terrier will vary on the amount of eye contact he can take and his ability to sustain it. Though short attention spans can be improved upon, this can be a taxing job. Eventually, the dog should graduate to eye contact at all distances when his name is called, or the owner is giving instructions.

PLAY TRAINING

Teaching a puppy through playing is the fastest and easiest way to teach a Jack Russell Terrier. Given a chance, a Jack Russell puppy will play, eat, sleep, then play some more. This dog considers hunting as valuable as play. Jack Russell puppies are easily distracted, but they always have a keen interest in playing. Mixing playing with learning helps the medicine go down.

One example of how to do this is with the "come" command. The owner can call the puppy's name, and say "come" enticingly and excitedly. If the puppy doesn't come, try patting the ground and asking again. When the puppy arrives, run away like a game of tag. Another technique is to throw a ball and yell "come" when the dog is going to come

anyway. You can get a partner to roll the ball back and forth to you. Always praise and give the puppy extra hugs when he does something asked for during play time. Using play with learning keeps the puppy from realizing he is in school.

SOCIALIZATION

It is good to expose Jack Russell Terrier puppies to people. Let the dog have good experience with humans outside the family and let him learn to be friendly. This will not in the least inhibit his devotion to the owner or family. When the time is taken to create the kind of early life bonding this terrier deeply desires, the dog will always first and foremost remain true to the owner. If relationship in marriages were as strong as the ones developed by Jack Russells and their owners, there'd never be a divorce. A well-socialized puppy that has begun his training early adds greatly to manageability. The first three to four months of your puppy's life

It is important to afford your Jack Russell plenty of opportunity to associate with other animals. "Ricki" enjoys the company of her daughter and granddaughter immensely.

Socialization is very important in the case of the Jack Russell Terrier. Make sure the puppy is used to being handled before bringing him home.

have a profound effect on how easy the dog will be to train. Since the JRTCA recommends dogs not be sold until eight weeks of age, the socialization efforts of the breeder are very important. Make sure the breeder has done his or her job in handling the young puppies before buying the dog. Be wary of purchasing older pups from production kennels or pet shops. These dogs may not have had the essential time alone with people. Also, although crate training is good to do at this age, do not over-crate the puppy. For the first six to ten weeks of life, dogs need to investigate and sort things out in their environment. They cannot do this if they are confined to a kennel or crate all day long. Excessive confinement at this time in their development can cause the dog to become unnaturally hyperactive.

Lack of bonding makes the dog indifferent to the owner. With this breed's tendencies to be convinced of his own importance, the owner compounds training difficulty when the dog is indifferent.

ADOLESCENCE

Adolescence is the most naughty time for dogs. The dog is more frisky, more aggressive, has highs and lows, is into everything, and at times can appear to have gone brain dead. Adolescence is a time when the dog will be testing the limits. Although adolescence passes for a lot of dogs after the first year, others will persist with some of their adolescent behavior until two years of age. Victory is a slow process with subtle rewards.

HOUSEBREAKING

The easiest way to housebreak your Jack Russell Terrier is to use the dog's natural times to eliminate to your advantage. Dogs by nature are den animals. They do not want to eliminate in the den where they sleep. When the owner trains the dog to go outside of his den (house) they are merely modifying what the dog does naturally. One of the things that affects the puppy's ability to be housebroken is that some pups have stronger muscle and bladder control than others. Control may also vary with age. The owner will find the task easier if the puppy is on a schedule. Feed the pup at the same time every day. Take the puppy outside:

Never confine your puppy to his crate as a form of punishment. Your Jack Russell Terrier should consider his crate a safe haven from the world.

1. When the puppy wakes up;
2. After feeding;
3. After play period or during play period if the play period is long;
4. If the pup has been inside for three or four hours without a break;
5. When the dog looks like he is looking for a place to go;
6. Before bedtime.

For a while it will seem as if the owner is the one who is trained. At first this is true. The owner will learn when to take the dog out at the right time for elimination. Eventually, the dog's natural instinct clicks in and a little light goes on inside the dog's head.

Paper training is one of the many methods used to housetrain a puppy.

A few ways to facilitate housebreaking is for the owner to train the dog to a certain area in the yard. This helps the dog get into the routine of going outside and getting right down to business. If the dog doesn't eliminate right away, then the owner needs to return to the house. Don't ever mix business with pleasure when housetraining your puppy. The dog is not to associate going out to eliminate as play time, or instead of the owner training his dog to get down to business when going outside for elimination, the dog will train the owner to take him outside to play.

Another trick that may help in training when the weather is cold is to carry the dog out to the place he needs to go. Puppies may not want to walk in the cold snow all the way out to the owner's selected area. Usually the selected area is far enough away from the house that if the puppy is set down

Training the dog to eliminate in a specific area of the yard often facilitates housetraining.

and has hesitation about eliminating, the walk back lets him know he doesn't get out of the cold any faster. If the dog does wait until he gets back to the warm house, the owner needs to transport both puppy and waste out to the outside elimination area. Make the puppy stand for a short while before letting him walk back to the house.

If the puppy does have an accident inside the house a firm "no" is plenty of punishment. Since the puppy will want to go where he has gone before, it is a good idea to disinfect the area inside the house where the accident happened. Water mixed with vinegar or a commercial product that masks the smell of the mess will do the job. Don't ever forget to praise when the puppy does it right.

CRATE TRAINING

Some Jack Russell Terrier owners have found that during the housebreaking stage, using a crate can help eliminate accidents. When the owner cannot watch the puppy, he should put the puppy in his crate. Every time the puppy comes

Crates make housetraining your pet much easier because dogs do not want to soil where they eat and sleep.

out of the crate, take him outside to eliminate. After the puppy has done his business, be sure to take some time and play. Play is a reward in itself.

Crating a dog is a good way of meeting the dog's natural instinct to have a den area of his own. Other advantages of crate training include the dog learning patience, learning to be quiet in the house, and to have a safe means of transportation to the veterinarian. Proper training can also facilitate housebreaking. Crate training should begin when the dog is a puppy.

The first thing to do is select a crate. Use one that will work when the puppy is grown, but still not be excessively large. A crate 26 inches deep and 16 inches high is a good size for an adult, but about as large as can be used for a puppy. Dogs like small dens and will instinctually want to keep it clean. Too large a crate will encourage the puppy to use one end as a bathroom.

Put the dog in the crate for about half an hour to start with. It's a good idea to give a treat when putting the puppy in to give him the idea that this is a good place to be. A good time to crate the puppy is right before nap time. Although chew sticks can be put in for entertainment, do not give puppies a lot of water until they are old enough to hold their urine. Puppies can also sleep at night in their crates until they are housebroken.

Do not let a puppy out of the crate when he is making a fuss about the confinement. Get the pup to quit whining or barking first, then let him out when he is quiet. Never use the crate as a punishment area. If the dog has misbehaved and needs confinement, a quiet room (make sure it is safe and that things are picked up and out of the way) with the lights off can be a better place to put the puppy. Confinement for punishment should only be for 10-30 minutes.

The dog's basic needs are not met when confined inside a small crate all day long. Signs of overcrating include the dog becoming hyperactive or self-destructive. Remember, any dog that has been crated for a long time needs to be exercised when he is let out.

THE COME COMMAND

All the training for the "come" command will be a waste of time if the dog doesn't see the owner as someone worth coming to. The dog must respect the owner as the boss—the undisputed leader of the pack. Because of the nature of the Jack Russell Terrier, this command is the toughest to teach. A Jack Russell is energetic, and he wants to do what he thinks is important without being interrupted by his owner, especially if he is hunting. Although

The "come" command is one of the most important lessons your dog will learn to ensure his safety and well being.

Basic obedience training is necessary for your puppy, not only to teach him acceptable behavior, but to keep him safe as well.

this is the toughest command to teach, looking at some guidelines for teaching the dog to come will help in training the Jack Russell in general.

The best time to start teaching the come command is when your Jack Russell is a puppy. Whatever command is used, the owner must be consistent with the term. Coax the dog over, or if the dog won't come, pull him to you on his leash. Give rewards and praise when the dog reaches you. Repeat until the dog responds to the command. Depending on the dog, this will take a few days to teach and a few weeks for him to consistently obey.

Once the dog is obeying the command *without fail* inside the house, move outside to a fenced area. Again the dog needs to get proficient at this command before being taken outside a confined area. The first time the dog is taken to an unconfined area, keep the Jack Russell on a long leash (20 feet or more). If the owner decides to use a retractable leash, eye gear (even as simple as sunglasses) is important. Retractable leashes have caused eye injury when they malfunction.

When the dog is attached to a long leash, the owner can let the dog wander away. After the dog is preoccupied, the owner can give the command to come. Use the dog's name before the command to catch the dog's attention. If the dog comes when called, reward him with a treat and/or a lot of praise. If the dog doesn't come, repeat the command, then a moment later give the leash a sharp jerk. Again repeat the command. If the dog still doesn't come, reel him in. Even though you had to reel in the dog, the dog should be rewarded when he gets to you, teaching him that there is reward in obedience.

Once the dog is coming consistently on the leash, it is time to take it off. Ask for the dog to come. If the dog does, reward him immediately. If the dog ignores the command, you can clap hands or try and get the dog's attention, then repeat the command. If the dog fails to come, never punish the dog when he finally is caught. Jack Russell Terriers are not stupid and punishment teaches the dog to be reluctant to be caught the next time.

Sometimes a dog learns that the owner, without the use of a leash, has limited control. A clever Jack Russell might take advantage of this. Some people have tried using shock collars to help. Usually the Jack Russell can figure out when the shock collar is and isn't on. For a shock collar to work, a dummy collar must be used or the Jack Russell will immediately pick up on when the collar is or isn't on and decide to come accordingly.

Some owners notice early success in come training (four to five months), only to find failure later on. This is sometimes due to an inadequately trained dog and sometimes due to the rebellion precipitated during adolescence. When the young dog reaches adolescence, he will stop responding unless the lesson is thoroughly taught by the owner and the owner convinces the dog that he must obey.

The owner must re-teach the come command in different situations. The worst thing an owner can do is assume that because the puppy comes in the backyard and the house that he will come when loose in the park or an unfenced area. A drag rope or long leash helps the owner to catch the dog and reel him in. Remember, always praise when the dog arrives, even if you pulled him all the way to you.

With Jack Russell Terriers, using a drag line may be something you need to do. When the trainers of the dog Eddie got him, the woman used a drag line to teach Eddie to come when called. She turned him loose one day, expecting he'd obey–after all, most dogs responded positively in that amount of time. She spent hours chasing him down. She didn't punish him, but put him back on the drag line for several more months until the dog came to the conclusion that he must obey. Understanding was not the issue.

PROOF TRAINING

Proof training involves training a dog to obey under any and all circumstances. The outline for training to come deals with proof training. Proof training is necessary, not because the dog doesn't understand what is wanted, but because the dog doesn't believe that the owner will require obedience all of the time.

The time you invest in training your Jack Russell Terriers will benefit them throughout their lifetime. Good training will surely allow them to live life to its fullest.

VICES

Digging and Chewing

Most behavior problems are caused by boredom and isolation and this type of undesirable behavior is spawned from the same place. Jack Russells were bred as a working and hunting dog. They are happiest as workaholics, and they are creative enough to find something to occupy themselves. Treating the cause, not the effect, is the true solution to these two problems. To correct either problem, first eliminate the cause with more exercise and play. If the problem doesn't go away, then follow up with a reprimand.

Aggression Towards Animals

The original Jack Russell was bred to flush out his prey. Around the turn of the century, some of the Jack Russells were bred to kill rats. Though in general the breed isn't geared towards violence, the dog will usually try to kill rodents like mice, rats, and small pets. Sometimes, especially when two terriers are together, the excitement of chasing something can turn into a killing frenzy. Unfortunately cats sometimes become victims. Even Jack Russells raised with cats have been known to attack them. Dominance, territorialism, and the hunting instinct all add a part of this problem. All Jack Russell owners must accept the fact that there is a possibility that they may not be able to keep a cat with their dog.

The general recommendation for keeping two Jack Russells of the same sex together is **do not.** Jack Russells have been known to kill each other when two of the same sex are kept together. A Jack Russell breeder had one female in heat crawl

Puppyhood displays of dominance are natural, however this same behavior in adulthood is not acceptable. A dominant pup will need a firm but fair owner.

over a four-foot fence and kill another female that was expecting puppies. Both sexes show aggression. There are some owners who can keep a kennel of Jack Russells together. This is no accident, nor is it luck. These owners are extremely good at asserting themselves with the dogs. This is a unique talent of knowing how much discipline, when to discipline, and the assertion of the owner as the indisputable leader of the pack. The owners must also ride shotgun on any squabbles that arise. The best recommendation is

Oftentimes, behavior problems like chewing are caused by boredom and isolation. Make sure your Jack Russell Terrier has plenty of toys to keep him occupied and away from your shoes!

not to plan on keeping two Jack Russells of the same sex together. Even dogs that have been raised together can turn on one another because of jealousy. Some people have had better luck keeping Jack Russells together that have been neutered or spayed. The general recommendation is that until owners know their Jack Russell well, they should not leave two together unattended. Many sad stories have been generated by owners who come home to discover a major fight has led to severe injuries or the death of one of the dogs.

Owning a Jack Russell Terrier demands the owner become a good trainer. Even with stacks of books from the library and the information in this chapter, some owners need help, and some dogs can present exceptional problems. There are times that calling in trained help will bring peace to the dog and owner. Some of the old schools of training depend too much on punishment for results. Be sure the trainer who is employed is exceptional and preferably experienced with Jack Russell Terriers. The JRTCA can be contacted at P. O. Box 4527, Lutherville, MD 21094 for help, recommendations and advice. Once the owner gets the knack of training his Jack Russell, he will find it fun and easy.

Finally, armed with a new beloved, well-trained Jack Russell, an owner can find a lot of fun and satisfaction in showing and working this breed.

SPORT of Purebred Dogs

Welcome to the exciting and sometimes frustrating sport of dogs. No doubt you are trying to learn more about dogs or you wouldn't be deep into this book. This section covers the basics that may entice you, further your knowledge and help you to understand the dog world.

Dog showing has been a very popular sport for a long time and has been taken quite seriously by some. Others only enjoy it as a hobby.

The Kennel Club in England was formed in 1859, the American Kennel Club was established in 1884 and the Canadian Kennel Club was formed in 1888. The purpose of these clubs was to register purebred dogs and maintain their Stud Books. In the beginning, the concept of registering dogs was

Handlers must wear comfortable practical clothing that does not distract attention from the dog they are showing.

not readily accepted. More than 36 million dogs have been enrolled in the AKC Stud Book since its inception in 1888. Presently the kennel clubs not only register dogs but adopt and enforce rules and regulations governing dog shows, obedience trials and field trials. Over the years they have fostered and encouraged interest in the health and welfare of the purebred dog. They routinely donate funds to veterinary research for study on genetic disorders.

Below are the addresses of the kennel clubs in the United States, Great Britain and Canada.

The American Kennel Club
51 Madison Avenue
New York, NY 10010
(Their registry is located at: 5580 Centerview Drive, STE 200, Raleigh, NC 27606-3390)

The Kennel Club
1 Clarges Street
Piccadilly, London, WIY 8AB,
England

The Canadian Kennel Club
111 Eglinton Avenue
East Toronto, Ontario M6S 4V7
Canada

Breed clubs often sponsor shows to showcase that breed's expertise. In the case of the Jack Russell Terrier, field trials are particularly popular.

Today there are numerous activities that are enjoyable for both the dog and the handler. Some of the activities include conformation showing, obedience competition, tracking, agility, the Canine Good Citizen Certificate, and a wide range of instinct tests that vary from breed to breed. Where you start depends upon your goals which early on may not be readily apparent.

Puppy Kindergarten

Every puppy will benefit from this class. PKT is the foundation for all future dog activities from conformation to "couch potatoes." Pet owners should make an effort to attend even if they never expect to show their dog. The class is designed for puppies about three months of age with graduation at approximately five months of age. All the puppies will be in the same age group and, even though some may be a little unruly, there should not be any real problem. This class will teach the puppy some beginning obedience. As in all obedience classes the owner learns how to train his own dog. The PKT class gives the puppy the opportunity to interact with other puppies in the same age group and exposes him to strangers, which is very important. Some dogs grow up with behavior problems, one of them being fear of strangers. As you can see, there can be much to gain from this class.

There are some basic obedience exercises that every dog should learn. Some of these can be started with puppy kindergarten.

Sit

One way of teaching the sit is to have your dog on your left side with the leash in your right hand, close to the collar. Pull up on the leash and at the same time reach around his hindlegs with your left hand and tuck them in. As you are doing this say, "Beau, sit." Always use the dog's name when you give an active command. Some owners like to use a treat holding it over the dog's head. The dog will need to sit to get the treat. Encourage the dog to hold the sit for a few seconds, which will eventually be the beginning of the Sit/Stay. Depending on how cooperative he is, you can rub him under the chin or stroke his back. It is a good time to establish eye contact.

Down

Sit the dog on your left side and kneel down beside him with the leash in your right hand. Reach over him with your left hand and grasp his left foreleg. With your right hand, take his right foreleg and pull his legs forward while you say, "Beau, down." If he tries to get up, lean on his shoulder to encourage him to stay down. It will relax your dog if you stroke his back while he is down. Try to encourage him to stay down for a few seconds as preparation for the Down/Stay.

Heel

The definition of heeling is the dog walking under control at your left heel. Your puppy will learn controlled walking in the puppy kindergarten class, which will eventually lead to heeling. The command is "Beau, heel," and you start off briskly with your left foot. Your leash is in your right hand and your left hand is holding it about half way down. Your left hand should be able to control the leash and there should be a little slack in it. You want him to walk with you with your leg somewhere between his nose and his shoulder. You need to encourage him to stay with you, not forging (in front of you) or lagging behind you. It is best to keep him on a fairly short lead. Do not allow the lead to become tight. It is far better to give him a little jerk when necessary and remind him to heel. When you come to a halt, be prepared physically to make him sit. It takes practice to become coordinated. There are excellent books on training that you may wish to purchase. Your instructor should be able to recommend one for you.

There are certain commands that every dog should know how to perform. Outback Keegan knows that practice makes perfect.

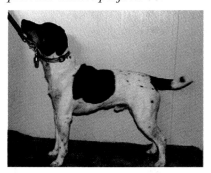

Recall

This quite possibly is the most important exercise you will ever teach. It should be a pleasant experience. The puppy may learn to do random recalls while being attached to a long line such as a clothes line. Later the exercise will start with the dog sitting and staying until called. The command is "Beau, come." Let your command be happy. You want your dog to come willingly and faithfully. The recall could save his life if he sneaks out the door. In practicing the recall, let him jump on you or touch you before you reach for him. If he is shy, then kneel down to his level. Reaching for the insecure dog could frighten him, and he may not be willing to come again in the future. Lots of praise and a treat would be in order whenever you do a recall. Under no circumstances should you ever correct your dog when he has come to you. Later in formal obedience your dog will be required to sit in front of you after recalling and then go to heel position.

CONFORMATION

Conformation showing is our oldest dog show sport. This type of showing is based on the dog's appearance—that is his structure, movement and attitude. When considering this type of showing, you need to be aware of your breed's standard and be able to evaluate your dog compared to that standard. The breeder of your puppy or other experienced breeders would be good sources for such an evaluation. Puppies can go through lots of changes over a period of time. Many puppies start out as promising hopefuls and then after maturing may be disappointing as show candidates. Even so this should not deter them from being excellent pets.

Usually conformation training classes are offered by the local kennel or obedience clubs. These are excellent places for training puppies. The puppy should be able to walk on a lead before entering such a class. Proper ring procedure and technique for posing (stacking) the dog will be demonstrated as well as gaiting the dog. Usually certain patterns are used in the ring such as the triangle or the "L." Conformation class, like the PKT class, will give your youngster the opportunity to socialize with different breeds of dogs and humans too.

It takes some time to learn the routine of conformation showing. Usually one starts at the puppy matches that may be AKC Sanctioned or Fun Matches. These matches are generally for puppies from two or three months to a year old, and there may be classes for the adult over the age of 12 months. Similar to point shows, the classes are divided by sex and after completion of the classes in that breed or variety, the class winners compete for Best of Breed or Variety. The winner goes on to compete in the Group and the Group winners compete for Best in Match. No championship points are awarded for match wins.

A few matches can be great training for puppies even though there is no intention to go on showing. Matches enable the puppy to meet new people and be handled by a stranger—the judge. It is also a change of environment, which broadens the horizon for both dog and handler. Matches and other dog activities boost the confidence of the handler and especially the younger handlers.

Earning an AKC championship is built on a point system, which is different from Great Britain. To become an AKC

Champion of Record the dog must earn 15 points. The number of points earned each time depends upon the number of dogs in competition. The number of points available at each show depends upon the breed, its sex and the location of the show. The United States is divided into ten AKC zones. Each zone has its own set of points. The purpose of the zones is to try to equalize the points available from breed to breed and area to area. The AKC adjusts the point scale annually.

The number of points that can be won at a show are between one and five. Three-, four- and five-point wins are considered majors. Not only does the dog need 15 points won under three different judges, but those points must include two majors under two different judges. Canada also works on a point system but majors are not required.

Dogs always show before bitches. The classes available to those seeking points are: Puppy (which may be divided into 6 to 9 months and 9 to 12 months); 12 to 18 months; Novice; Bred-by-Exhibitor; American-bred; and Open. The class winners of the same sex of each breed or variety

In conformation your dog is judged by how closely he conforms to the standard of the breed.

99

compete against each other for Winners Dog and Winners Bitch. A Reserve Winners Dog and Reserve Winners Bitch are also awarded but do not carry any points unless the Winners win is disallowed by AKC. The Winners Dog and Bitch compete with the specials (those dogs that have attained championship) for Best of Breed or Variety, Best of Winners and Best of Opposite Sex. It is possible to pick up an extra point or even a major if the points are higher for the defeated winner than those of Best of Winners. The latter would get the higher total from the defeated winner.

At an all-breed show, each Best of Breed or Variety winner will go on to his respective Group and then the Group winners will compete against each other for Best in Show. There are seven Groups: Sporting, Hounds, Working, Terriers, Toys, Non-Sporting and Herding. Obviously there are no Groups at speciality shows (those shows that have only one breed or a show such as the American Spaniel Club's Flushing Spaniel Show, which is for all flushing spaniel breeds).

Earning a championship in England is somewhat different since they do not have a point system. Challenge Certificates are awarded if the judge feels the dog is deserving regardless of the number of dogs in competition. A dog must earn three Challenge Certificates under three different judges, with at least one of these Certificates being won after the age of 12 months. Competition is very strong and entries may be higher than they are in the U.S. The Kennel Club's Challenge Certificates are only available at Championship Shows.

Successful showing requires dedication and preparation, but most of all, it should be an enjoyable experience for handlers and dogs alike.

In England, The Kennel Club regulations require that certain dogs, Border Collies and Gundog breeds, qualify in a working capacity (i.e., obedience or field trials) before becoming a full Champion. If they do not qualify in the working aspect, then they are designated a Show Champion, which is equivalent to the AKC's Champion of Record. A Gundog may be granted the title of Field Trial Champion (FT

There are so many activities that you and your dog can participate in and the versatile Jack Russell Terrier has the ability to excel at them all.

With persistence, patience, and praise, your versatile Jack Russell Terrier puppy will become a well-trained and obedient companion.

Ch.) if it passes all the tests in the field but would also have to qualify in conformation before becoming a full Champion. A Border Collie that earns the title of Obedience Champion (Ob Ch.) must also qualify in the conformation ring before becoming a Champion.

The U.S. doesn't have a designation full Champion but does award for Dual and Triple Champions. The Dual Champion must be a Champion of Record, and either Champion Tracker, Herding Champion, Obedience Trial Champion or Field Champion. Any dog that has been awarded the titles of Champion of Record, and any two of the following: Champion Tracker, Herding Champion, Obedience Trial Champion or Field Champion, may be designated as a Triple Champion.

Crating your dog is a safe way to transport your Jack Russell from show to show.

The shows in England seem to put more emphasis on breeder judges than those in the U.S. There is much competition within the breeds. Therefore the quality of the individual breeds should be very good. In the United States we tend to have more "all around judges" (those that judge multiple breeds) and use the breeder judges at the specialty shows. Breeder judges are more familiar with their own breed since they are actively breeding that breed or did so at one time. Americans emphasize Group and Best in Show wins and promote them accordingly.

The shows in England can be very large and extend over several days, with the Groups being scheduled on different days. Though multi-day shows are not common in the U.S., there are cluster shows, where several different clubs will use the same show site over consecutive days.

Westminster Kennel Club is our most prestigious show although the entry is limited to 2500. In recent years, entry has been limited to Champions. This show is more formal than the majority of the shows with the judges wearing formal attire and the handlers fashionably

It is difficult for a breeder to tell if her Jack Russell's will be "show quality" dogs much before four months of age. Even if these pups are not, they'll still make great pets.

103

dressed. In most instances the quality of the dogs is superb. After all, it is a show of Champions. It is a good show to study the AKC registered breeds and is by far the most exciting–especially since it is televised! WKC is one of the few shows in this country that is still benched. This means the dog must be in his benched area during the show hours except when he is being groomed, in the ring, or being exercised.

Typically, the handlers are very particular about their appearances. They are careful not to wear something that will detract from their dog but will perhaps enhance it. American ring procedure is quite formal compared to that of other countries. There is a certain etiquette expected between the judge and exhibitor and among the other exhibitors. Of course it is not always the case but the judge is supposed to be polite, not engaging in small talk or acknowledging how well he knows the handler. There is a more informal and relaxed atmosphere at the shows in other countries. For instance, the dress code is more casual. I can see where this might be more fun for the exhibitor and especially for the novice. The U.S. is very handler-oriented in many of the breeds. It is true, in most instances, that the experienced professional handler can present the dog better and will have a feel for what a judge likes.

In England, Crufts is The Kennel Club's own show and is most assuredly the largest dog show in the world. They've been known to have an entry of nearly 20,000, and the show lasts four days. Entry is only gained by qualifying through winning in specified classes at another Championship Show. Westminster is strictly conformation, but Crufts exhibitors and spectators

The chest span of a Jack Russell Terrier is very important in conformation class. Cheryl Robson and "Wedge" face the judges.

enjoy not only conformation but obedience, agility and a multitude of exhibitions as well. Obedience was admitted in 1957 and agility in 1983.

If you are handling your own dog, please give some consideration to your apparel. For sure the dress code at matches is more informal than the point shows. However, you should wear something a little more appropriate than beach attire or ragged jeans and bare feet. If you check out the handlers and see what is presently fashionable, you'll catch on. Men usually dress with a shirt and tie and a nice sports coat. Whether you are male or female, you will want to wear comfortable clothes

Handlers must pose their show dogs in the most flattering position to emphasize the dog's specific strengths and hide any flaws.

and shoes. You need to be able to run with your dog and you certainly don't want to take a chance of falling and hurting yourself. Heaven forbid, if nothing else, you'll upset your dog. Women usually wear a dress or two-piece outfit, preferably with pockets to carry bait, comb, brush, etc. In this case men are the lucky ones with all their pockets. Ladies, think about where your dress will be if you need to kneel on the floor and also think about running. Does it allow freedom to do so?

You need to take along dog; crate; ex pen (if you use one); extra newspaper; water pail and water; all required grooming equipment, including hair dryer and extension cord; table; chair for you; bait for dog and lunch for you and friends; and, last but not least, clean up materials, such as plastic bags, paper towels, and perhaps a bath towel and some shampoo— just in case. Don't forget your entry confirmation and directions to the show.

If you are showing in obedience, then you will want to wear pants. Many of our top obedience handlers wear pants that are color-coordinated with their dogs. The philosophy is that imperfections in the black dog will be less obvious next to your black pants.

Whether you are showing in conformation, Junior Showmanship or obedience, you need to watch the clock and be sure you are not late. It is customary to pick up your

Pat Scanlan and his Jack Russell Terrier "Dillon" show off their many ribbons from wins at various shows.

conformation armband a few minutes before the start of the class. They will not wait for you and if you are on the show grounds and not in the ring, you will upset everyone. It's a little more complicated picking up your obedience armband if you show later in the class. If you have not picked up your armband and they get to your number, you may not be allowed to show. It's best to pick up your armband early, but then you may show earlier than expected if other handlers don't pick up. Customarily all conflicts should be discussed with the judge prior to the start of the class.

Junior Showmanship

The Junior Showmanship Class is a wonderful way to build self-confidence even if there are no aspirations of staying with the dog-show game later in life. Frequently, Junior Showmanship becomes the background of those who become successful exhibitors/handlers in the future. In some instances it is taken very seriously, and success is measured in terms of wins. The Junior Handler is judged solely on his ability and skill in presenting his dog. The dog's conformation is not to be considered by the judge. Even so the condition and grooming of the dog may be a reflection upon the handler.

Usually the matches and point shows include different classes. The Junior Handler's dog may be entered in a breed or obedience class and even shown by another person in that class. Junior Showmanship classes are usually divided by age and perhaps sex. The age is determined by the handler's age on the day of the show. The classes are:

Novice Junior for those at least ten and under 14 years of age who at time of entry closing have not won three first places in a Novice Class at a licensed or member show.

Excelling in obedience competition is easy for working dogs like the Jack Russell Terrier that are used to following orders from their masters.

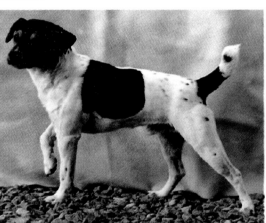

Novice Senior for those at least 14 and under 18 years of age who at the time of entry closing have not won three first places in a Novice Class at a licensed or member show.

Open Junior for those at least ten and under 14 years of age who at the time of entry closing have won at least three first places in a Novice Junior Showmanship Class at a licensed or member show with competition present.

Open Senior for those at least 14 and under 18 years of age who at time of entry closing have won at least three first places in a Novice Junior Showmanship Class at a licensed or member show with competition present.

Junior Handlers must include their AKC Junior Handler number on each show entry. This needs to be obtained from the AKC.

CANINE GOOD CITIZEN

The AKC sponsors a program to encourage dog owners to train their dogs. Local clubs perform the pass/fail tests, and dogs who pass are awarded a Canine Good Citizen Certificate. Proof of vaccination is required at the time of participation. The test includes:

Obedience training requires that your Jack Russell heed your commands, even when he is playing with his favorite toy!

1. Accepting a friendly stranger.
2. Sitting politely for petting.
3. Appearance and grooming.
4. Walking on a loose leash.
5. Walking through a crowd.
6. Sit and down on command/staying in place.
7. Come when called.
8. Reaction to another dog.
9. Reactions to distractions.
10. Supervised separation.

If more effort was made by pet owners to accomplish these exercises, fewer dogs would be cast off to the humane shelter.

OBEDIENCE

Obedience is necessary, without a doubt, but it can also become a wonderful hobby or even an obsession. Obedience classes and competition can provide wonderful companionship, not only with your dog but with your classmates or fellow competitors. It is always gratifying to discuss your dog's problems with others who have had similar experiences. The AKC acknowledged Obedience around 1936, and it has changed tremendously even though many of the exercises are basically the same. Today, obedience competition is just that—very competitive. Even so, it is possible for every obedience exhibitor to come home a winner (by earning qualifying scores) even though he/she may not earn a placement in the class.

Canine good citizens must be able to get along well with other animals. These Jack Russells look as if they've passed the test.

Most of the obedience titles are awarded after earning three qualifying scores (legs) in the appropriate class under three different judges. These classes offer a perfect score of 200, which is extremely rare. Each of the class exercises has its own point value. A leg is earned after receiving a score of at least 170 and at least 50 percent of the points available in each exercise. The titles are:

The intelligent and inquisitive Jack Russell Terrier excels in obedience training and enjoys pleasing his master.

Companion Dog–CD
This is called the Novice Class and the exercises are:

1. Heel on leash and figure 8	40 points
2. Stand for examination	30 points
3. Heel free	40 points
4. Recall	30 points
5. Long sit—one minute	30 points
6. Long down—three minutes	30 points

Maximum total score   200 points

Companion Dog Excellent–CDX
This is the Open Class and the exercises are:

1. Heel off leash and figure 8	40 points
2. Drop on recall	30 points
3. Retrieve on flat	20 points
4. Retrieve over high jump	30 points
5. Broad jump	20 points
6. Long sit—three minutes (out of sight)	30 points
7. Long down—five minutes (out of sight)	30 points

Maximum total score   200 points

Utility Dog–UD
The Utility Class exercises are:

1. Signal Exercise	40 points
2. Scent discrimination-Article 1	30 points
3. Scent discrimination-Article 2	30 points
4. Directed retrieve	30 points
5. Moving stand and examination	30 points
6. Directed jumping	40 points
Maximum total score	200 points

After achieving the UD title, you may feel inclined to go after the UDX and/or OTCh. The UDX (Utility Dog Excellent) title went into effect in January 1994. It is not easily attained. The title requires qualifying simultaneously ten times in Open B and Utility B but not necessarily at consecutive shows.

The OTCh (Obedience Trial Champion) is awarded after the dog has earned his UD and then goes on to earn 100 championship points, a first place in Utility, a first place in Open and another first place in either class. The placements must be won under three different judges at all-breed obedience trials. The points are determined by the number of dogs competing in the Open B and Utility B classes. The OTCh title precedes the dog's name.

Agility is just one of the many activities in which Jack Russell Terriers can demonstrate their athletic and competitive prowess.

Obedience matches (AKC Sanctioned, Fun, and Show and Go) are usually available. Usually they are sponsored by the local obedience clubs. When preparing an obedience dog for a title, you will find matches very helpful. Fun Matches and Show and Go Matches are more lenient in allowing you to make corrections in the ring. This type of training is usually very necessary for the Open and Utility Classes. AKC Sanctioned Obedience Matches do not allow corrections in the ring since they must abide by the AKC Obedience Regulations. If you are interested in showing in obedience, then you should contact the AKC for a copy of the Obedience Regulations.

AGILITY

Agility was first introduced by John Varley in England at the Crufts Dog Show, February 1978, but Peter Meanwell, competitor and judge, actually developed the idea. It was officially recognized in the early '80s. Agility is extremely popular in England and Canada and growing in popularity in the U.S. The AKC acknowledged agility in August 1994. Dogs

Agility competition is growing in popularity. This Jack Russell Terrier easily completes a tunnel simulation activity.

must be at least 12 months of age to be entered. It is a fascinating sport that the dog, handler and spectators enjoy to the utmost. Agility is a spectator sport! The dog performs off lead. The handler either runs with his dog or positions himself on the course and directs his dog with verbal and hand signals over a timed course over or through a variety of obstacles including a time out or pause. One of the main drawbacks to agility is finding a place to train. The obstacles take up a lot of space and it is very time consuming to put up and take down courses.

The titles earned at AKC agility trials are Novice Agility Dog (NAD), Open Agility Dog (OAD), Agility Dog Excellent (ADX), and Master Agility Excellent (MAX). In order to acquire an agility title, a dog must earn a qualifying score in its respective class on three separate occasions under two different judges.

The MAX will be awarded after earning ten qualifying scores in the Agility Excellent Class.

PERFORMANCE TESTS

During the last decade the American Kennel Club has promoted performance tests–those events that test the different breeds' natural abilities. This type of event encourages a handler to devote even more time to his dog and retain the natural instincts of his breed heritage. It is an important part of the wonderful world of dogs.

Earthdog Events

For small terriers (Australian, Bedlington, Border, Cairn, Dandie Dinmont, Fox (Smooth & Wire), Lakeland, Norfolk, Norwich, Scottish, Sealyham, Skye, Welsh, West Highland White and Dachshunds).

Limited registration (ILP) dogs are eligible and all entrants must be at least six months of age. The primary purpose of the small terriers and Dachshunds is to pursue quarry to ground, hold the game, and alert the hunter where to dig, or to bolt. There are two parts to the test: (1) the approach to the quarry and (2) working the quarry. The dog must pass both parts for a Junior Earthdog (JE). The Senior Earthdog (SE) must do a third part–to leave the den on command. The Master Earthdog (ME) is a bit more complicated.

GENERAL INFORMATION

Obedience, tracking and agility allow the purebred dog with an Indefinite Listing Privilege (ILP) number or a limited registration to be exhibited and earn titles. Application must be made to the AKC for an ILP number.

The American Kennel Club publishes a monthly *Events* magazine that is part of the *Gazette*, their official journal for the sport of purebred dogs. The *Events* section lists upcoming shows and the secretary or superintendent for them. The majority of the conformation shows in the U.S. are overseen by licensed superintendents. Generally the entry closing date is approximately two-and-a-half weeks before the actual show. Point shows are fairly expensive, while the match shows cost about one third of the point show entry fee. Match shows usually take entries the day of the show but some are pre-entry.

The best way to find match show information is through your local kennel club. Upon asking, the AKC can provide you with a list of superintendents, and you can write and ask to be put on their mailing lists.

Obedience trial and tracking test information is available through the AKC. Frequently these events are not superintended, but put on by the host club. Therefore you would make the entry with the event's secretary.

As you have read, there are numerous activities you can share with your dog. Regardless what you do, it does take teamwork. Your dog can only benefit from your attention and training. We hope this chapter has enlightened you and hope, if nothing else, you will attend a show here and there. Perhaps you will start with a puppy kindergarten class, and who knows where it may lead!

Training for any type of competition or activity allows the owner and his dog to develop a closeness through working together. This owner retrieves her Jack Russell Terrier from the end of a Go-To-Ground training course.

HEALTH CARE

Veterinary medicine has become far more sophisticated than what was available to our ancestors. This can be attributed to the increase in household pets and consequently the demand for better care for them. Also human medicine has become far more complex. Today diagnostic testing in veterinary medicine parallels human diagnostics. Because of better technology we can expect our pets to live healthier lives thereby increasing their life spans.

THE FIRST CHECK UP

You will want to take your new puppy/dog in for its first check up within 48 to 72 hours after acquiring it. Many breeders strongly recommend this check up and so do the humane shelters. A puppy/dog can appear healthy but it may have a serious problem that is not apparent to the layman. Most pets have some type of a minor flaw that may never cause a real problem.

Jack Russell Terrier's require some vegetable matter in their diet. The CARROT BONE™, made by Nylabone®, helps control plaque, eases the need to chew, and is nutritious. It is highly recommended as a healthy toy for your Jack Russell Terrier.

For the sake of your puppy as well as the health of your family, you should bring your new Jack Russell Terrier to the veterinarian within three days of his arrival at your home.

Unfortunately if he/she should have a serious problem, you will want to consider the consequences of keeping the pet and the attachments that will be formed, which may be broken prematurely. Keep in mind there are many healthy dogs looking for good homes.

This first check up is a good time to establish yourself with the veterinarian and learn the office policy regarding their hours and how they handle emergencies. Usually the breeder or another conscientious pet owner is a good reference for locating a capable veterinarian. You should be aware that not all veterinarians give the same quality of service. Please do not make your selection on the least expensive clinic, as they may be shortchanging your pet. There is the possibility that eventually it will cost you more due to improper diagnosis, treatment, etc. If you are selecting a new veterinarian, feel free to ask for a tour of the clinic. You should inquire about making an appointment for a tour since all clinics are working clinics, and therefore may not be available all day for sightseers. You may worry less if you see where your pet will be spending the day if he ever needs to be hospitalized.

THE PHYSICAL EXAM

Your veterinarian will check your pet's overall condition, which includes listening to the heart; checking the respiration; feeling the abdomen, muscles and joints; checking the mouth, which includes the gum color and signs of gum disease along with plaque buildup; checking the ears for signs of an infection or ear mites; examining the eyes; and, last but not least, checking the condition of the skin and coat.

He should ask you questions regarding your pet's eating and elimination habits and invite you to relay your questions. It is a good idea to prepare a list so as not to forget anything. He should discuss the proper diet and the quantity to be fed. If this should differ from your breeder's recommendation, then you should convey to him the breeder's choice and see if he approves. If he recommends changing the diet, then this should be done over a few days so as not to cause a gastrointestinal upset. It is customary to take in a fresh stool sample (just a small amount) for a test for intestinal parasites. It must be fresh, preferably within 12 hours, since the eggs hatch quickly and after hatching will not be observed under the microscope. If your pet isn't obliging then, usually the technician can take one in the clinic.

IMMUNIZATIONS

It is important that you take your puppy/dog's vaccination record with you on your first visit. In case of a puppy, presumably the breeder has seen to the vaccinations up to the time you acquired custody. Veterinarians differ in their vaccination protocol. It is not unusual for your puppy to have received vaccinations for distemper, hepatitis, leptospirosis, parvovirus and parainfluenza every two to three weeks from the age of five or six weeks. Usually this is a combined injection and is typically called the DHLPP. The DHLPP is given through at least 12 to 14 weeks of age, and it is customary to continue with another parvovirus vaccine at 16 to 18 weeks. You may wonder why so many immunizations are necessary. No one knows for sure when the puppy's maternal antibodies are gone, although it is customarily accepted that distemper antibodies are gone by 12 weeks. Usually parvovirus antibodies are gone by 16 to 18 weeks of age. However, it is possible for the maternal antibodies to be gone at a much earlier age or even a later age. Therefore immunizations are started at an early age. The vaccine will not give immunity as long as there are maternal antibodies.

The rabies vaccination is given at three or six months of age depending on your local laws. A vaccine for bordetella (kennel cough) is advisable and can be given anytime from the age of five weeks. The coronavirus is not commonly given unless there is a problem locally. The Lyme vaccine is necessary in endemic areas. Lyme disease has been reported in 47 states.

Distemper

This is virtually an incurable disease. If the dog recovers, he is subject to severe nervous disorders. The virus attacks every tissue in the body and resembles a bad cold with a fever. It can cause a runny nose and eyes and cause gastrointestinal disorders, including a poor appetite, vomiting and diarrhea. The virus is carried by raccoons, foxes, wolves, mink and other dogs. Unvaccinated youngsters and senior citizens are very susceptible. This is still a common disease.

Hepatitis

This is a virus that is most serious in very young dogs. It is spread by contact with an infected animal or its stool or urine. The virus affects the liver and kidneys and is characterized by high fever, depression and

Check your Jack Russell Terrier's coat carefully after he has been playing outside for any external parasites like fleas or ticks.

lack of appetite. Recovered animals may be afflicted with chronic illnesses.

Leptospirosis

This is a bacterial disease transmitted by contact with the urine of an infected dog, rat or other wildlife. It produces severe symptoms of fever, depression, jaundice and internal bleeding and was fatal before the vaccine was developed. Recovered dogs can be carriers, and the disease can be transmitted from dogs to humans.

Parvovirus

This was first noted in the late 1970s and is still a fatal disease. However, with proper vaccinations, early diagnosis and prompt treatment, it is a manageable disease. It attacks the bone marrow and intestinal tract. The symptoms include depression, loss of appetite, vomiting, diarrhea and collapse. Immediate medical attention is of the essence.

Rabies

This is shed in the saliva and is carried by raccoons, skunks, foxes, other dogs and cats. It attacks nerve tissue, resulting in paralysis and death. Rabies can be transmitted to people and is virtually always fatal. This disease is reappearing in the suburbs.

Bordetella (Kennel Cough)

The symptoms are coughing, sneezing, hacking and retching

A healthy and tasty treat for your Jack Russell Terrier because they love cheese is CHOOZ™. CHOOZ™ are bone-hard but can be microwaved to expand into a huge, crispy dog biscuit. They are almost fat free and about 70% protein.

accompanied by nasal discharge usually lasting from a few days to several weeks. There are several disease-producing organisms responsible for this disease. The present vaccines are helpful but do not protect for all the strains. It usually is not life threatening but in some instances it can progress to a serious bronchopneumonia. The disease is highly contagious. The vaccination should be given routinely for dogs that come in contact with other dogs, such as through boarding, training class or visits to the groomer.

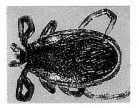

The deer tick is the most common carrier of Lyme disease. Photo courtesy of Virbac Laboratories, Inc., Fort Worth, Texas.

Coronavirus

This is usually self limiting and not life threatening. It was first noted in the late '70s about a year before parvovirus. The virus produces a yellow/brown stool and there may be depression, vomiting and diarrhea.

Lyme Disease

This was first diagnosed in the United States in 1976 in Lyme, CT in people who lived in close proximity to the deer tick. Symptoms may include acute lameness, fever, swelling of joints and loss of appetite. Your veterinarian can advise you if you live in an endemic area.

After your puppy has completed his puppy vaccinations, you will continue to booster the DHLPP once a year. It is customary to booster the rabies one year after the first vaccine and then, depending on where you live, it should be boostered every year or every three years. This depends on your local laws. The Lyme and corona vaccines are boostered annually and it is recommended that the bordetella be boostered every six to eight months.

Annual Visit

I would like to impress the importance of the annual check up, which would include the booster vaccinations, check for intestinal parasites and test for heartworm. Today in our very busy world it is rush, rush and see "how much you can get for

how little." Unbelievably, some non-veterinary businesses have entered into the vaccination business. More harm than good can come to your dog through improper vaccinations, possibly from inferior vaccines and/or the wrong schedule. More than likely you truly care about your companion dog and over the years you have devoted much time and expense to his well being. Perhaps you are unaware that a vaccination is not just a vaccination. There is more involved. Please, please follow through with regular physical examinations. It is so important for your veterinarian to know your dog and this is especially true during middle age through the geriatric years. More than likely your older dog will require more than one physical a year.

Roundworm eggs, as would be seen on a fecal evaluation. The eggs must develop for at least 12 days before they are infectious.

The annual physical is good preventive medicine. Through early diagnosis and subsequent treatment your dog can maintain a longer and better quality of life.

INTESTINAL PARASITES

Hookworms

These are almost microscopic intestinal worms that can cause anemia and therefore serious problems, including death, in young puppies. Hookworms can be transmitted to humans through penetration of the skin. Puppies may be born with them.

Roundworms

These are spaghetti-like worms that can cause a potbellied appearance and dull coat along with more severe symptoms, such as vomiting, diarrhea and coughing. Puppies acquire these while in the mother's uterus and through lactation. Both hookworms and roundworms may be acquired through ingestion.

Regular medical care is just as important for the adult Jack Russell Terrier as it is for the puppy. Vaccination boosters and physical exams are part of your dog's lifelong maintenance.

Whipworms

These have a three-month life cycle and are not acquired through the dam. They cause intermittent diarrhea usually with mucus. Whipworms are possibly the most difficult worm to eradicate. Their eggs are very resistant to most environmental factors and can last for years until the proper conditions enable them to mature. Whipworms are seldom seen in the stool.

Intestinal parasites are more prevalent in some areas than others. Climate, soil and contamination are big factors contributing to the incidence of intestinal parasites. Eggs are passed in the stool, lay on the ground and then become infective in a certain number of days. Each of the above worms has a different life cycle. Your best chance of becoming and remaining worm-free is to always pooper-scoop your yard. A fenced-in yard keeps stray dogs out, which is certainly helpful.

Whipworms are hard to find, and it is a job best left to a veterinarian. Pictured here are adult whipworms.

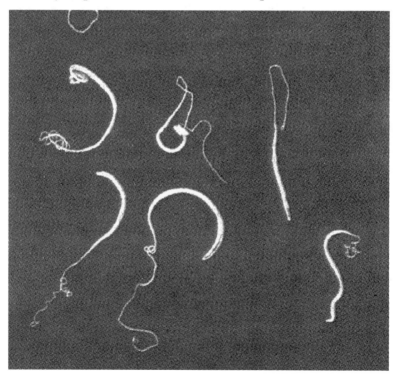

I would recommend having a fecal examination on your dog twice a year or more often if there is a problem. If your dog has a positive fecal sample, then he will be given the appropriate medication and you will be asked to bring back another stool sample in a certain period of time (depending on the type of worm) and then be rewormed. This process goes on until he has at least two negative samples. The different types of worms require different medications. You will be wasting your money and doing your dog an injustice by buying over-the-counter medication without first consulting your veterinarian.

OTHER INTERNAL PARASITES

Coccidiosis and Giardiasis

These protozoal infections usually affect puppies, especially in places where large numbers of puppies are brought together. Older dogs may harbor these infections but do not show signs unless they are stressed. Symptoms include diarrhea, weight loss and lack of appetite. These infections are not always apparent in the fecal examination.

Dirofilaria—*adult worms in the heart of a dog. Courtesy of Merck Ag Vet.*

Tapeworms

Seldom apparent on fecal floatation, they are diagnosed frequently as rice-like segments around the dog's anus and the base of the tail. Tapeworms are long, flat and ribbon like, sometimes several feet in length, and made up of many segments about five-eighths of an inch long. The two most common types of tapeworms found in the dog are:

(1) First the larval form of the flea tapeworm parasite must mature in an intermediate host, the flea, before it can become infective. Your dog acquires this by ingesting the flea through licking and chewing.

(2) Rabbits, rodents and certain large game animals serve as intermediate hosts for other species of tapeworms. If your dog should eat one of these infected hosts, then he can acquire tapeworms.

125

HEARTWORM DISEASE

This is a worm that resides in the heart and adjacent blood vessels of the lung that produces microfilaria, which circulate in the bloodstream. It is possible for a dog to be infected with any number of worms from one to a hundred that can be 6 to 14 inches long. It is a life-threatening disease, expensive to treat and easily prevented. Depending on where you live, your veterinarian may recommend a preventive year-round and either an annual or semiannual blood test. The most common preventive is given once a month.

EXTERNAL PARASITES

Fleas

These pests are not only the dog's worst enemy but also enemy to the owner's pocketbook. Preventing is less expensive than treating, but regardless we'd prefer to spend our money elsewhere. Likely, the majority of our dogs are allergic to the bite of a flea, and in many cases it only takes one flea bite. The protein in the flea's saliva is the culprit. Allergic dogs have a reaction, which usually results in a "hot spot." More than likely such a reaction will involve a trip to the veterinarian for treatment. Yes, prevention is less expensive. Fortunately today there are several good products available.

If there is a flea infestation, no one product is going to correct the problem. Not only will the dog require treatment so will the environment. In general, flea collars are not very effective although there is now available an "egg" collar that will kill the eggs on the dog. Dips are the most economical but they are messy. There are some effective shampoos and treatments available through pet shops and veterinarians. An oral tablet arrived on the American market in 1995 and was popular in Europe the previous year. It sterilizes the female flea but will not kill adult fleas. Therefore the tablet, which is given monthly, will decrease the flea population but is not a "cure-all." Those dogs that suffer from flea-bite allergy will still be subjected to the bite of the flea. Another popular parasiticide is permethrin, which is applied to the back of the dog in one or two places depending on the dog's weight. This product works as a repellent causing the flea to get "hot feet" and jump off. Do not confuse this product with some of the organophosphates that are also applied to the dog's back.

Some products are not usable on young puppies. Treating fleas should be done under your veterinarian's guidance. Frequently it is necessary to combine products and the layman does not have the knowledge regarding possible toxicities. It is hard to believe but there are a few dogs that do have a natural resistance to fleas. Nevertheless it would be wise to treat all pets at the same time. Don't forget your cats. Cats just love to prowl the neighborhood and consequently return with unwanted guests.

The cat flea is the most common flea of both dogs and cats. It starts feeding soon after it makes contact with the dog.

Adult fleas live on the dog but their eggs drop off the dog into the environment. There they go through four larval stages before reaching adulthood, and thereby are able to jump back on the poor unsuspecting dog. The cycle resumes and takes between 21 to 28 days under ideal conditions. There are environmental products available that will kill both the adult fleas and the larvae.

Ticks

Ticks carry Rocky Mountain Spotted Fever, Lyme disease and can cause tick paralysis. They should be removed with tweezers, trying to pull out the head. The jaws carry disease. There is a tick preventive collar that does an excellent job. The ticks automatically back out on those dogs wearing collars.

Sarcoptic Mange

This is a mite that is difficult to find on skin scrapings. The pinnal reflex is a good indicator of this disease. Rub the ends of the pinna (ear) together and the dog will start scratching with his foot. Sarcoptes are highly contagious to other dogs and to humans although they do not live long on humans. They cause intense itching.

Demodectic Mange

This is a mite that is passed from the dam to her puppies. It affects youngsters age three to ten months. Diagnosis is confirmed by skin scraping. Small areas of alopecia around the eyes, lips and/or forelegs become visible. There is little itching unless there is a secondary bacterial infection. Some breeds are afflicted more than others.

Cheyletiella

This causes intense itching and is diagnosed by skin scraping. It lives in the outer layers of the skin of dogs, cats, rabbits and humans. Yellow-gray scales may be found on the back and the rump, top of the head and the nose.

To Breed or Not To Breed

More than likely your breeder has requested that you have your puppy neutered or spayed. Your breeder's request is based on what is healthiest for your dog and what is most beneficial for your breed. Experienced and conscientious breeders devote many years into developing a bloodline. In order to do this, he makes every effort to plan each breeding in regard to conformation, temperament and health. This type of breeder does his best to perform the necessary testing (i.e., OFA, CERF, testing for inherited blood disorders, thyroid, etc.). Testing is expensive and sometimes very disheartening when a favorite dog doesn't pass his health tests. The health history pertains not only to the breeding stock but to the immediate ancestors. Reputable breeders do not want their offspring to

There are all kinds of flying disks for dogs, but only one is made with strength, scent, and originality. The Nylabone® Frisbee™ is a must if you want to have this sort of fun with your Jack Russell Terrier. The trademark frisbee is used under license from Mattel, Inc., California, USA.

be bred indiscriminately. Therefore you may be asked to neuter or spay your puppy. Of course there is always the exception, and your breeder may agree to let you breed your dog under his direct supervision. This is an important concept. More and more effort is being made to breed healthier dogs.

The HERCULES™ is made of very tough polyurethane. It is designed for Jack Russell Terriers who are extremely strong chewers. The raised dental tips massage the gums and mechanically remove the plaque they encounter during chewing.

Breeding dogs of only the best quality assures that good health and temperament are passed down to each new generation.

Spay/ Neuter

There are numerous benefits of performing this surgery at six months of age. Unspayed females are subject to mammary and ovarian cancer. In order to prevent mammary cancer she must be spayed prior

to her first heat cycle. Later in life, an unspayed female may develop a pyometra (an infected uterus), which is definitely life threatening.

Spaying is performed under a general anesthetic and is easy on the young dog. As you might expect it is a little harder on the older dog, but that is no reason to deny her the surgery. The surgery removes the ovaries and uterus. It is important to remove all the ovarian tissue. If some is left behind, she could remain attractive to males. In order to view the ovaries, a reasonably long incision is necessary. An ovariohysterectomy is considered major surgery.

Neutering the male at a young age will inhibit some characteristic male behavior that owners frown upon. Some boys will not hike their legs and mark territory if they are neutered at six months of age. Also neutering at a young age has hormonal benefits, lessening the chance of hormonal aggressiveness.

Surgery involves removing the testicles but leaving the scrotum. If there should be a retained testicle, then he definitely needs to be neutered before the age of two or three years. Retained testicles can develop into cancer. Unneutered males are at risk for testicular cancer, perineal fistulas, perianal tumors and fistulas and prostatic disease.

POPpup's™ are healthy treats for your Jack Russell Terrier. When bone-hard they help to control plaque build-up; when microwaved they become a rich cracker which your Jack Russell will love. The POPpup™ is available in liver and other flavors and is fortified with calcium.

All Jack Russell Terrier puppies are cute, but not all are of breeding quality. Reputable breeders will often sell pet-quality pups on the condition that they are spayed or neutered.

Intact males and females are prone to housebreaking accidents. Females urinate frequently before, during and after heat cycles, and males tend to mark territory if there is a female in heat. Males may show the same behavior if there is a visiting dog or guests.

Surgery involves a sterile operating procedure equivalent to human surgery. The incision site is shaved, surgically scrubbed and draped. The veterinarian wears a sterile surgical gown, cap, mask and gloves. Anesthesia should be monitored by a registered technician. It is customary for the veterinarian to recommend a pre-anesthetic blood screening, looking for metabolic problems and an ECG rhythm strip to check for normal heart function. Today anesthetics are equal to human anesthetics, which enables your dog to walk out of the clinic the same day as surgery.

Some folks worry about their dog gaining weight after being neutered or spayed. This is usually not the case. It is true that some dogs may be less active so they could develop a problem, but most dogs are just as active as they were before surgery. However, if your dog should begin to gain weight, then you need to decrease his food and see to it that he gets a little more exercise.

DENTAL CARE for Your Dog's Life

So you've got a new puppy! You also have a new set of puppy teeth in your household. Anyone who has ever raised a puppy is abundantly aware of these new teeth. Your puppy will chew anything it can reach, chase your shoelaces, and play "tear the rag" with any piece of clothing it can find. When puppies are newly born, they have no teeth. At about four weeks of age, puppies of most breeds begin to develop their deciduous or baby teeth. They begin eating semi-solid food, fighting and biting with their litter mates, and learning discipline from their mother. As their new teeth come in, they inflict more pain on their mother's breasts, so her feeding sessions become less frequent and shorter. By six or eight weeks, the mother will start growling to warn her pups when they are fighting too roughly or hurting her as they nurse too much with their new teeth.

Puppies need to chew. It is a necessary part of their physical and mental development. They develop muscles and necessary life skills as they drag objects around, fight over possession, and vocalize alerts and warnings. Puppies chew on things to explore their world. They are using their sense of taste to determine what is food and what is not. How else can they tell an electrical cord from a lizard? At about four months of age, most puppies begin shedding their baby teeth. Often these teeth need some help to come out and make way for the permanent teeth. The incisors (front teeth) will be replaced first. Then, the adult canine or fang teeth erupt. When the baby tooth is not shed before the permanent tooth comes in, veterinarians call it a retained deciduous tooth. This condition will often cause gum infections by trapping hair and debris between the permanent tooth and the retained baby tooth. Nylafloss® is an excellent device for puppies to use. They can toss it, drag it, and chew on the many surfaces it presents. The baby teeth can catch in the nylon material, aiding in their removal. Puppies that have adequate chew toys will have less destructive behavior, develop more physically, and have less chance of retained deciduous teeth.

During the first year, your dog should be seen by your veterinarian at regular intervals. Your veterinarian will let you know when to bring in your puppy for vaccinations and parasite examinations. At each visit, your veterinarian should inspect the lips, teeth, and mouth as part of a complete physical examination. You should take some part in the maintenance of your dog's oral health. You should examine your dog's mouth weekly throughout his first year to make sure there are no sores, foreign objects, tooth problems, etc. If your dog drools excessively, shakes his head, or has bad breath, consult your veterinarian. By the time your dog is six months old, the permanent teeth are all in and plaque can start to accumulate on the tooth surfaces. This is when your dog needs to develop good dental-care habits to prevent calculus build-up on his teeth. Brushing is best. That is a fact that cannot be denied. However, some dogs do not like their teeth brushed regularly, or you may not be able to accomplish the task. In that case, you should consider a product that will help prevent plaque and calculus build-up.

There is only one material suitable for flossing human teeth and that's nylon. So why not get a chew toy that will enable you to interact with your Jack Russell Terrier while it promotes dental health. As you play tug-of-war with a NYLAFLOSS®, you'll be slowly pulling the nylon strands through your dog's teeth.

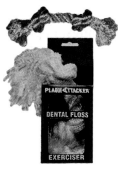

The Plaque Attackers® and Galileo Bone® are other excellent choices for the first three years of a dog's life. Their shapes make them interesting for the dog. As the dog chews on them, the solid polyurethane massages the gums which improves the blood circulation to the periodontal tissues. Projections on the chew devices increase the surface and are in contact with the tooth for more efficient cleaning. The unique shape and consistency prevent your dog from exerting excessive force on his own teeth or from breaking off pieces of the bone. If your dog is an aggressive chewer or weighs more than 55 pounds (25 kg), you should consider giving him a Nylabone®, the most durable chew product on the market.

The Gumabones ®, made by the Nylabone Company, is constructed of strong polyurethane, which is softer than nylon. Less powerful chewers prefer the Gumabones® to the Nylabones®. A super option for your dog is the Hercules Bone®, a uniquely shaped bone named after the great Olympian for its exceptional strength. Like all Nylabone products, they are specially scented to make them attractive to your dog. Ask your veterinarian about these bones and he will validate the good doctor's prescription: Nylabones® not only give your dog a good chewing workout but also help to save your dog's teeth (and even his life, as it protects him from possible fatal periodontal diseases).

By the time dogs are four years old, 75% of them have periodontal disease. It is the most common infection in dogs. Yearly examinations by your veterinarian are essential to maintaining your dog's good health. If your veterinarian detects periodontal disease, he or she may recommend a prophylactic cleaning. To do a thorough cleaning, it will be necessary to put your dog under anesthesia. With modern gas anesthetics and monitoring equipment, the procedure is pretty safe. Your veterinarian will scale the teeth with an ultrasound scaler or hand instrument. This removes the calculus from the teeth. If there are calculus deposits below the gum line, the veterinarian will plane the roots to make them smooth. After all of the calculus has been removed, the teeth are polished with pumice in a polishing cup. If any medical or surgical treatment is needed, it is done at this time. The final step would be fluoride treatment and your follow-up treatment at home. If the periodontal disease is advanced, the veterinarian may prescribe a medicated mouth rinse or antibiotics for use at home. Make sure your dog has safe, clean and attractive chew toys and treats. Chooz® treats are another way of using a consumable treat to help keep your dog's teeth clean.

A thorough examination of your Jack Russell Terriers mouth, teeth, and gums should be part of his annual check-up.

Rawhide is the most popular of all materials for a dog to chew. This has never been good news to dog owners, because rawhide is inherently very dangerous for dogs. Thousands of dogs have died from rawhide, having swallowed the hide after it has become soft and mushy, only to cause stomach and intestinal blockage. A new rawhide product on the market has finally solved the problem of rawhide: molded Roar-Hide® from Nylabone. These are composed of processed, cut up, and melted American rawhide injected into your dog's favorite shape: a dog bone. These dog-safe devices smell and taste like rawhide but don't break up. The ridges on the bones help to fight tartar build-up on the teeth and they last ten times longer than the usual rawhide chews.

Brushing your dog's teeth is recommended by every veterinarian. Use the 2-Brush® regularly, 3-4 times per week, and you may never need your veterinarian to do the job for you.

As your dog ages, professional examination and cleaning should become more frequent. The mouth should be inspected at least once a year. Your veterinarian may recommend visits every six months. In the geriatric patient, organs such as the heart, liver, and kidneys do not function as well as when they were young. Your veterinarian will probably want to test these organs' functions prior to using general anesthesia for dental cleaning. If your dog is a good chewer and you work closely with your veterinarian, your dog can keep all of his teeth all of his life. However, as your dog ages, his sense of smell, sight, and taste will diminish. He may not have the desire to chase, trap or chew his toys. He will also not have the energy to chew for long periods, as arthritis and periodontal disease make chewing painful. This will leave you with more responsibility for keeping his teeth clean and healthy. The dog that would not let you brush his teeth at one year of age, may let you brush his teeth now that he is ten years old.

If you train your dog with good chewing habits as a puppy, he will have healthier teeth throughout his life.

TRAVELING with Your Dog

The earlier you start traveling with your new puppy or dog, the better. He needs to become accustomed to traveling. However, some dogs are nervous riders and become carsick easily. It is helpful if he starts with an empty stomach. Do not despair, as it will go better if you continue taking him with you on short fun rides. How would you feel if every time you rode in the car you stopped at the doctor's for an injection? You would soon dread that nasty car. Older dogs that tend to get carsick may have more of a problem adjusting to traveling. Those dogs that are having a serious problem may benefit from some medication prescribed by the veterinarian.

Jack Russell Terriers are active dogs and will enjoy traveling with you wherever you go. This guy looks ready for some sun and fun!

Do give your dog a chance to relieve himself before getting into the car. It is a good idea to be prepared for a clean up with a leash, paper towels, bag and terry cloth towel.

The safest place for your dog is in a fiberglass crate, although close confinement can promote carsickness in some dogs. If your dog is nervous you can try letting him ride on the seat next to you or in someone's lap.

An alternative to the crate would be to use a car harness made for dogs and/or a safety strap attached to the harness or collar. Whatever you do, do not let your dog ride in the back of a pickup truck unless he is securely tied on a very short lead. I've seen trucks stop quickly and, even though the dog was tied, he fell out and was dragged.

Before any car excursion, be sure your Jack Russell is allowed plenty of time outdoors to attend to his needs.

Another advantage of the crate is that it is a safe place to leave him if you need to run into the store. Otherwise you wouldn't be able to leave the windows down. Keep in mind that while many dogs are overly protective in their crates, this may not be enough to deter dognappers. In some states it is against the law to leave a dog in the car unattended.

Never leave a dog loose in the car wearing a collar and leash. More than one dog has killed himself by hanging. Do not let him put his head out an open window. Foreign debris can be blown into his eyes. When leaving your dog unattended in a car, consider the temperature. It can take less than five minutes to reach temperatures over 100 degrees Fahrenheit.

TRIPS

Perhaps you are taking a trip. Give consideration to what is best for your dog—traveling with you or boarding. When traveling by car, van or motor home, you need to think ahead about locking your vehicle. In all probability you have many valuables in the car and do not wish to leave it unlocked. Perhaps most valuable and not replaceable is your dog. Give thought to securing your vehicle and providing adequate ventilation for him. Another consideration for you when traveling with your dog is medical problems that may arise and little inconveniences, such as exposure to external parasites. Some areas of the country are quite flea infested. You may want to carry flea spray with you. This is even a good idea when staying in motels. Quite possibly you are not the only occupant of the room.

Unbelievably many motels and even hotels do allow canine guests, even some very first-class ones. Gaines Pet Foods Corporation publishes *Touring With Towser*, a directory of domestic hotels and motels that accommodate guests with dogs. Their address is Gaines TWT, PO Box 5700, Kankakee, IL, 60902. Call ahead to any motel that you may be considering and see if they accept pets. Sometimes it is necessary to pay a deposit against room damage. The management may feel reassured if you mention that your dog will be crated. If you do travel with your dog, take along plenty of baggies so that you can clean up after him. When we all do our share in cleaning up, we make it possible for motels to continue accepting our pets. As a matter of fact, you should practice cleaning up everywhere you take your dog.

Depending on where you are traveling, you may need an up-to-date health certificate issued by your veterinarian. It is good policy to take along your dog's medical information, which would include the name, address and phone number of your veterinarian, vaccination record, rabies certificate, and any medication he is taking.

AIR TRAVEL

When traveling by air, you need to contact the airlines to check their policy. Usually you have to make arrangements up to a couple of weeks in advance for traveling with your dog. The airlines

If you decide to bring your Jack Russell Terrier with you when you travel, bring along some familiar things, like his bed and toys, to make him feel more at home.

Crates are a safe way for your dog to travel. The fiberglass crates are the safest for air travel, but the metal crates allow for better air circulation.

require your dog to travel in an airline approved fiberglass crate. Usually these can be purchased through the airlines but they are also readily available in most pet-supply stores. If your dog is not accustomed to a crate, then it is a good idea to get him acclimated to it before your trip. The day of the actual trip you should withhold water about one hour ahead of departure and no food for about 12 hours. The airlines generally have temperature restrictions, which do not allow pets to travel if it is either too cold or too hot. Frequently these restrictions are based on the temperatures at the departure and arrival airports. It's best to inquire about a health certificate. These usually need to be issued within ten days of departure. You should arrange for non-stop, direct flights and if a commuter plane should be involved, check to see if it will carry dogs. Some don't. The Humane Society of the United States has put together a tip sheet for airline traveling. You can receive a copy by sending a self-addressed stamped envelope to:

The Humane Society of the United States
Tip Sheet
2100 L Street NW
Washington, DC 20037.

Regulations differ for traveling outside of the country and are sometimes changed without notice. Well in advance you need to write or call the appropriate consulate or agricultural department for instructions. Some countries have lengthy quarantines (six months), and countries differ in their rabies vaccination requirements. For instance, it may have to be given at least 30 days ahead of your departure.

Do make sure your dog is wearing proper identification including your name, phone number and city. You never know when you might be in an accident and separated from your dog. Or your dog could be frightened and somehow manage to escape and run away.

Your puppy's well being is important to you, so be sure to inquire about airline and hotel regulations before making travel plans.

Another suggestion would be to carry in-case-of-emergency instructions. These would include the address and phone number of a relative or friend, your veterinarian's name, address and phone number, and your dog's medical information.

BOARDING KENNELS

Perhaps you have decided that you need to board your dog. Your veterinarian can recommend a good boarding facility or possibly a pet sitter that will come to your house. It is customary for the boarding kennel to ask for proof of vaccination for the DHLPP, rabies and bordetella vaccine. The bordetella should have been given within six months of boarding. This is for your protection. If they do not ask for this proof I would not board at their kennel. Ask about flea control. Those dogs that suffer flea-bite allergy can get in trouble at a boarding kennel. Unfortunately boarding kennels are limited on how much they are able to do.

Make sure your Jack Russell Terrier wears a collar with tags at all times. This will increase your chances of being reunited should you become separated.

For more information on pet sitting, contact NAPPS:
National Association of Professional Pet Sitters
1200 G Street, NW
Suite 760
Washington, DC 20005.

Some pet clinics have technicians that pet sit and technicians that board clinic patients in their homes. This may be an alternative for you. Ask your veterinarian if they have an employee that can help you. There is a definite advantage of having a technician care for your dog, especially if your dog is on medication or is a senior citizen.

You can write for a copy of *Traveling With Your Pet* from ASPCA, Education Department, 441 E. 92nd Street, New York, NY 10128.

IDENTIFICATION and Finding the Lost Dog

There are several ways of identifying your dog. The old standby is a collar with dog license, rabies, and ID tags. Unfortunately collars have a way of being separated from the dog and tags fall off. We're not suggesting you shouldn't use a collar and tags. If they stay intact and on the dog, they are the quickest way of identification.

For several years owners have been tattooing their dogs. Some tattoos use a number with a registry. Here lies the problem because there are several registries to check. If you wish to tattoo, use your social security number. The humane shelters have the means to trace it. It is usually done on the inside of the rear thigh. The area is first shaved and numbed. There is no pain, although a few dogs do not like the buzzing sound. Occasionally tattooing is not legible and needs to be redone.

The newest method of identification is microchipping. The microchip is a computer chip that is no larger than a grain of rice. The veterinarian implants it by injection between the shoulder blades. The dog feels no discomfort. If your dog is lost and picked up by the humane society, they can trace you by scanning the microchip, which has its own code. Microchip scanners are friendly to other brands of microchips and their registries. The microchip comes with a dog tag saying the dog is microchipped. It is the safest way of identifying your dog.

FINDING THE LOST DOG

I am sure you will agree that there would be little worse than losing your dog. Responsible pet owners rarely lose their dogs. They do not let their dogs run free because they don't want harm to come to them. Not only that but in most, if not all, states there is a leash law.

Beware of fenced-in yards. They can be a hazard. Dogs find ways to escape either over or under the fence. Another fast exit is through the gate that perhaps the neighbor's child left unlocked.

Below is a list that hopefully will be of help to you if you need it. Remember don't give up, keep looking. Your dog is worth your efforts.

1. Contact your neighbors and put flyers with a photo on it in their mailboxes. Information you should include would be the dog's name, breed, sex, color, age, source of identification, when your dog was last seen and where, and your name and phone numbers. It may be helpful to say the dog needs medical care. Offer a *reward*.

2. Check all local shelters daily. It is also possible for your dog to be picked up away from home and end up in an out-of-the-way shelter. Check these too. Go in person. It is not good enough to call. Most shelters are limited on the time they can hold dogs then they are put up for adoption or euthanized. There is the possibility that your dog will not make it to the shelter for several days. Your dog could have been wandering or someone may have tried to keep him.

Make sure you have a clear recent picture of your dog to distribute in case he becomes lost.

3. Notify all local veterinarians. Call and send flyers.

4. Call your breeder. Frequently breeders are contacted when one of their breed is found.

5. Contact the rescue group for your breed.

6. Contact local schools—children may have seen your dog.

7. Post flyers at the schools, groceries, gas stations, convenience stores, veterinary clinics, groomers and any other place that will allow them.

8. Advertise in the newspaper.

9. Advertise on the radio.

BEHAVIOR and Canine Communication

S tudies of the human/animal bond point out the importance of the unique relationships that exist between people and their pets. Those of us who share our lives with pets understand the special part they play through companionship, service and protection. For many, the pet/owner bond goes beyond simple companionship; pets are often considered members of the family. A leading pet food manufacturer recently conducted a nationwide survey of pet owners to gauge just how important pets were in their lives. Here's what they found:

- 76 percent allow their pets to sleep on their beds
- 78 percent think of their pets as their children
- 84 percent display photos of their pets, mostly in their homes
- 84 percent think that their pets react to their own emotions
- 100 percent talk to their pets
- 97 percent think that their pets understand what they're saying

Are you surprised?

Jack Russell Terriers possess innate curiosity and can climb their way into all sorts of predicaments. Be sure to supervise your pup at all times.

Senior citizens show more concern for their own eating habits when they have the responsibility of feeding a dog. Seeing that their dog is routinely exercised encourages the owner to think of schedules that otherwise may seem unimportant to the senior citizen. The older owner

may be arthritic and feeling poorly but with responsibility for his dog he has a reason to get up and get moving. It is a big

Young people make great playmates for an energetic Jack Russell and caring for a dog will teach a child responsibility and respect for animals.

144

plus if his dog is an attention seeker who will demand such from his owner.

Over the last couple of decades, it has been shown that pets relieve the stress of those who lead busy lives. Owning a pet has been known to lessen the occurrence of heart attack and stroke.

Many single folks thrive on the companionship of a dog. Lifestyles are very different from a long time ago, and today more individuals seek the single life. However, they receive fulfillment from owning a dog.

Most likely the majority of our dogs live in family environments. The companionship they provide is well worth the effort involved. In my opinion, every child should have the opportunity to have a family dog. Dogs teach responsibility through

Dogs are a very important part of their owner's lives, and the bond between humans and animals is a strong one.

If you teach your Jack Russell Terrier proper behavior as a puppy, he will be able to accompany you anywhere—even on carriage rides!

understanding their care, feelings and even respecting their life cycles. Frequently those children who have not been exposed to dogs grow up afraid of dogs, which isn't good. Dogs sense timidity and some will take advantage of the situation.

Today more dogs are serving as service dogs. Since the origination of the Seeing Eye dogs years ago, we now have trained hearing dogs. Also dogs are trained to provide service for the handicapped and are able to perform many different tasks for their owners. Search and Rescue dogs, with their handlers, are sent throughout the world to assist in recovery of disaster victims. They are life savers.

Therapy dogs are very popular with nursing homes, and some hospitals even allow them to visit. The inhabitants truly look forward to their visits. They wanted and were allowed to have visiting dogs in their beds to hold and love.

Nationally there is a Pet Awareness Week to educate students and others about the value and basic care of our pets. Many countries take an even greater interest in their pets than Americans do. In those countries the pets are allowed to accompany their owners into restaurants and shops, etc. In the U.S. this freedom is only available to our service dogs. Even so we think very highly of the human/animal bond.

Canine Behavior

Canine behavior problems are the number-one reason for pet owners to dispose of their dogs, either through new homes, humane shelters or euthanasia. Unfortunately there are too many owners who are unwilling to devote the necessary time to properly train their dogs. On the other hand, there are those who not only are concerned about inherited health problems but are also aware of the dog's mental stability.

You may realize that a breed and his group relatives (i.e., sporting, hounds, etc.) show tendencies to behavioral characteristics. An experienced breeder can acquaint you with his breed's personality. Unfortunately many breeds are labeled with poor temperaments when actually the breed as a whole is not affected but only a small percentage of individuals within the breed.

Inheritance and environment contribute to the dog's behavior. Some naïve people suggest inbreeding as the cause of bad temperaments. Inbreeding only results in poor behavior if the ancestors carry the trait. If there are excellent temperaments behind the dogs, then inbreeding will promote good temperaments in the offspring. Did you ever consider that inbreeding is what sets the characteristics of a breed? A purebred dog is the end result of inbreeding. This does not spare the mixed-breed dog from the same problems. Mixed-breed dogs frequently are the offspring of purebred dogs.

Not too many decades ago most of our dogs led a different lifestyle than what is prevalent today. Usually mom stayed home so the dog had human companionship and someone to discipline it if needed. Not much was expected from the dog. Today's mom works and everyone's life is at a much faster pace.

The dog may have to adjust to being a "weekend" dog. The family is gone all day during the week, and the dog is left to his own devices for entertainment. Some dogs sleep all day waiting for their family to come home and others become wigwam wreckers if given the opportunity. Crates do ensure the safety of the dog and the house. However, he could become a physical and emotional cripple if he doesn't get enough exercise and attention. We still appreciate and want the companionship of our dogs although we expect more from them. In many cases we tend to forget dogs are just that—*dogs* not human beings.

SOCIALIZING AND TRAINING

Many prospective puppy buyers lack experience regarding the proper socialization and training needed to develop the type of pet we all desire. In the first 18 months, training does take some work. It is easier to start proper training before there is a problem that needs to be corrected.

The GALILEO™ is the toughest nylon bone ever made. It is flavored to appeal to your Jack Russell Terrier and has a relatively soft outer layer. It is a necessary chew toy and doggy pacifier. However, they are only useful if implemented carefully.

The initial work begins with the breeder. The breeder should start socializing the puppy at five to six weeks of age and cannot let up. Human socializing is critical up through 12 weeks of age and likewise important during the following months. The litter should be left together during the first few weeks but it is necessary to separate them by ten weeks of age. Leaving them together after that time will increase competition for litter dominance. If puppies are not socialized with people by 12 weeks of age, they will be timid in later life.

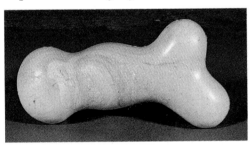

The eight- to ten-week age period is a fearful time for puppies. They need to be handled very gently around children and adults. There should be no harsh discipline during this time. Starting at 14 weeks of age, the puppy begins the juvenile period, which ends when he reaches sexual maturity around six to 14 months of age. During the juvenile period he needs to be introduced to strangers (adults, children and other dogs) on the home property. At sexual maturity he will begin to bark at strangers and become more protective. Males start to lift their legs to urinate but if you desire you can inhibit this behavior by walking your boy on leash away from trees, shrubs, fences, etc.

Perhaps you are thinking about an older puppy. You need to inquire about the puppy's social experience. If he has lived in a kennel, he may have a hard time adjusting to people and environmental stimuli. Assuming he has had a good social upbringing, there are advantages to an older puppy.

Although some traits are inherited within a breed, every Jack Russell Terrier is an individual with his own personality.

Training includes puppy kindergarten and a minimum of one to two basic training classes. During these classes you will learn how to dominate your youngster. This is especially important if you own a large breed of dog. It is somewhat harder, if not nearly impossible, for some owners to be the Alpha figure when their dog towers over them. You will be taught how to properly restrain your dog. This concept is important. Again it puts you in the Alpha position. All dogs need to be restrained many times during their lives. Believe it or not, some of our worst offenders are the eight-week-old puppies that are brought to our clinic. They need to be gently restrained for a nail trim but the way they carry on you would think we were killing them. In comparison, their vaccination is a "piece of cake." When we ask dogs to do something that is not agreeable to them, then their worst comes out. Life will be easier for your dog if you expose him at a young age to the necessities of life—proper behavior and restraint.

UNDERSTANDING THE DOG'S LANGUAGE

Most authorities agree that the dog is a descendent of the wolf.

A lot can be learned about a puppy's behavior and attitude simply by observing his body language. Determination is written all over this pup's face!

The dog and wolf have similar traits. For instance both are pack oriented and prefer not to be isolated for long periods of time. Another characteristic is that the dog, like the wolf, looks to the leader–Alpha–for direction. Both the wolf and the dog communicate through body language, not only within their pack but with outsiders.

Every pack has an Alpha figure. The dog looks to you, or should look to you, to be that leader. If your dog doesn't receive the proper training and guidance, he very well may replace you as Alpha. This would be a serious problem and is certainly a disservice to your dog.

Eye contact is one way the Alpha wolf keeps order within his pack. You are Alpha so you must establish eye contact with your puppy. Obviously your puppy will have to look at you. Practice eye contact even if you need to hold his head for five to ten seconds at a time. You can give him a treat as a reward. Make sure your eye contact is gentle and not threatening. Later, if he has been naughty, it is permissible to give him a long, penetrating look. There are some older dogs that never learned eye contact as puppies and cannot accept eye contact. You should avoid eye contact with these dogs since they feel threatened and will retaliate as such.

BODY LANGUAGE

The play bow, when the forequarters are down and the hindquarters are elevated, is an invitation to play. Puppies play fight, which helps them learn the acceptable limits of biting. This is necessary for later in their lives. Nevertheless, an owner may be falsely reassured by the playful nature of his dog's aggression. Playful aggression toward another dog or human may be an indication of serious aggression in the future.

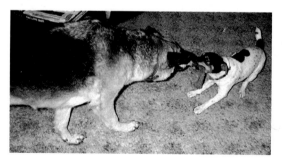

The Jack Russell possesses the courage and ego of a dog twice his size. Only a Jack Russell would think he could win this tug-of-war!

Owners should never play fight or play tug-of-war with any dog that is inclined to be dominant.

Signs of submission are:

1. Avoids eye contact.
2. Active submission—the dog crouches down, ears back and the tail is lowered.

3. Passive submission—the dog rolls on his side with his hindlegs in the air and frequently urinates.

A well-socialized Jack Russell will not be threatened by you approaching his food dish.

Eye contact is an extremely important aspect of your relationship with your Jack Russell Terrier. It will help to establish you as pack leader in your dog's mind.

Signs of dominance are:

1. Makes eye contact.
2. Stands with ears up, tail up and the hair raised on his neck.
3. Shows dominance over another dog by standing at right angles over it.

Dominant dogs tend to behave in characteristic ways such as:

1. The dog may be unwilling to move from his place (i.e., reluctant to give up the sofa if the owner wants to sit there).
2. He may not part with toys or objects in his mouth and may show possessiveness with his food bowl.
3. He may not respond quickly to commands.
4. He may be disagreeable for grooming and dislikes to be petted.

Behavior and health problems can be passed down from generation to generation, so be sure to check your puppy's lineage very carefully.

Dogs are popular because of their sociable nature. Those that have contact with humans during the first 12 weeks of life regard them as a member of their own species—their pack. All dogs have the potential for both dominant and submissive behavior. Only through experience and training do they learn to whom it is appropriate to show which behavior. Not all dogs are concerned with dominance but owners need to be aware of that potential. It is wise for the owner to establish his dominance early on.

A human can express dominance or submission toward a dog in the following ways:

1. Meeting the dog's gaze signals dominance. Averting the gaze signals submission. If the dog growls or threatens, averting the gaze is the first avoiding action to take—it may prevent attack. It is important to establish eye contact in the puppy. The

Puppies will find mischief whenever possible! For the safety of your dog and your belongings, supervise your Jack Russell at all times.

older dog that has not been exposed to eye contact may
see it as a threat and will not be willing to submit.

2. Being taller than the dog signals dominance; being
lower signals submission. This is why, when attempting to
make friends with a strange dog or catch the runaway, one
should kneel down to his level. Some owners see their
dogs become dominant when allowed on the furniture or
on the bed. Then he is at the owner's level.

3. An owner can gain dominance by ignoring all the dog's
social initiatives. The owner pays attention to the dog only
when he obeys a command.

No dog should be allowed to achieve dominant status over
any adult or child. Ways of preventing are as follows:

1. Handle the puppy gently, especially during the three-
to four-month period.

2. Let the children and adults handfeed him and teach
him to take food without lunging or grabbing.

3. Do not allow him to chase children or joggers.

4. Do not allow him to jump on people or mount their
legs. Even females may be inclined to mount. It is not only
a male habit.

5. Do not allow him to growl for any reason.

6. Don't participate in wrestling or tug-of-war games.

7. Don't physically punish puppies for aggressive
behavior. Restrain him from repeating the infraction and
teach an alternative behavior. Dogs should earn everything
they receive from their owners. This would include sitting
to receive petting or treats, sitting before going out the
door and sitting to receive the collar and leash. These
types of exercises reinforce the owner's dominance.

Young children should never be left alone with a dog. It is
important that children learn some basic obedience commands
so they have some control over the dog. They will gain the
respect of their dog.

Fear

One of the most common problems dogs experience is
being fearful. Some dogs are more afraid than others. On the
lesser side, which is sometimes humorous to watch, dogs can
be afraid of a strange object. They act silly when something is
out of place in the house. We call his problem perceptive

intelligence. He realizes the abnormal within his known environment. He does not react the same way in strange environments since he does not know what is normal.

On the more serious side is a fear of people. This can result in backing off, seeking his own space and saying "leave me alone" or it can result in an aggressive behavior that may lead to challenging the person. Respect that the dog wants to be left alone and give him time to come forward. If you approach the cornered dog, he may resort to snapping. If you leave him alone, he may decide to come forward, which should be rewarded with a treat.

Some dogs may initially be too fearful to take treats. In these cases it is helpful to make sure the dog hasn't eaten for about 24 hours. Being a little hungry encourages him to accept the treats, especially if they are of the "gourmet" variety.

Raised dental tips help to combat plaque and tartar on the surface of every Plaque Attacker™ bone. They are safe for aggressive chewers and ruggedly constructed to last.

Dogs can be afraid of numerous things, including loud noises and thunderstorms. Invariably the owner rewards (by comforting) the dog when it shows signs of fearfulness. When your dog is frightened, direct his attention to something else and act happy. Don't dwell on his fright.

AGGRESSION

Some different types of aggression are: predatory, defensive, dominant, possessive, protective, fear induced, noise provoked, "rage" syndrome (unprovoked aggression), maternal and aggression directed toward other dogs. Aggression is the most common behavioral problem encountered. Protective breeds are expected to be more aggressive than others but with the proper upbringing they can make very dependable companions. You need to be able to read your dog.

Many factors contribute to aggression including genetics and environment. An improper environment, which may include the living conditions, lack of social life, excessive punishment,

157

being attacked or frightened by an aggressive dog, etc., can all influence a dog's behavior. Even spoiling him and giving too much praise may be detrimental. Isolation and the lack of human contact or exposure to frequent teasing by children or adults also can ruin a good dog.

Lack of direction, fear, or confusion lead to aggression in those dogs that are so inclined. Any obedience exercise, even the sit and down, can direct the dog and overcome fear and/or confusion. Every dog should learn these commands as a youngster, and there should be periodic reinforcement.

When a dog is showing signs of aggression, you should speak calmly (no screaming or hysterics) and firmly give a command that he understands, such as the sit. As soon as your dog obeys, you have assumed your dominant position. Aggression presents a problem because there may be danger to others. Sometimes it is an emotional issue. Owners may consciously or unconsciously encourage their dog's aggression. Other owners show responsibility by accepting the problem and taking measures to keep it under control. The owner is responsible for his dog's actions, and it is not wise to take a chance on someone being bitten, especially a child. Euthanasia is the solution for some owners and in severe cases this may be the best choice. However, few dogs are that dangerous and very few are that much of a threat to their owners. If caution is exercised and professional help is gained early on, most cases can be controlled.

Some authorities recommend feeding a lower protein (less than 20 percent) diet. They believe this can aid in reducing aggression. If the dog loses weight, then vegetable oil can be added. Veterinarians and behaviorists are having some success with pharmacology. In many cases treatment is possible and can improve the situation.

If you have done everything according to "the book" regarding training and socializing and are still having a behavior problem, don't procrastinate. It is important that the problem gets attention before it is out of hand. It is estimated that 20 percent of a veterinarian's time may be devoted to dealing with problems before they become so intolerable that the dog is separated from his home and owner. If your veterinarian isn't able to help, he should refer you to a behaviorist.

SUGGESTED READING

TS-249
Skin and Coat Care for Your Dog
432 pages, over 300 full-color photos

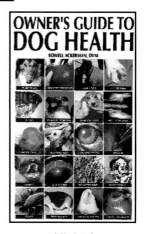

TS-214
Owner's Guide to Dog Health
224 pages, over 190 full-color photos

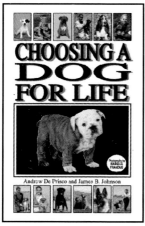

TS-257
Choosing a Dog for Life
384 pages, over 700 full-color photos.

TS-252
Dog Behavior and Training
292 pages, over 200 full-color photos

INDEX